KING
ARTHUR

KING ARTHUR

CHRISTOPHER HIBBERT

Consultant
Charles Thomas
Professor of Archaeology,
University of Leicester

This edition first published 2007
Published by arrangement with ibooks inc.
Tempus Publishing Limited
The Mill, Brimscombe Port,
Stroud, Gloucestershire, GL5 2QG
www.tempus-publishing.com

© American Heritage Inc. 1969, 2004, 2007

Originally published under the title *The Search for King Arthur.*

"The Quest for the Holy Grail" by Edwin Austin Abbey reproduced
courtesy of the Trustees of the Boston Public Library.

"The Quest for the Holy Grail" is Property of of the Trustees of the
Boston Public Library.

British Library Cataloguing in Publication Data.
A catalogue record for this book is available from the British Library.

ISBN 978 07524 3933 4

Typesetting and origination by Tempus Publishing Limited
Printed and bound in Great Britain

Contents

Foreword

The romances about King Arthur and his Knights of the Round Table are probably the best-known legends in the Western world. For most of us they have served as an introduction to the world of chivalry–of knights errant seeking honor and glory on difficult quests, of beauteous ladies watching their lovers joust in brilliant tournaments. It is a world that seems far removed from our own technologically advanced but uncertain times.

The true fascination of the Arthurian legend lies in the fact that their hero is not a myth but an actual historical figure who lived on the island of Britain some fourteen centuries ago in times that were, like our own, full of threats. With the crumbling of the Roman Empire, the people of Britain found themselves conducting a desperate defense of their island against Saxon invaders from across the North Sea. The pagan Saxons killed, looted, and burned; eventually, they took over larger and larger areas and gradually destroyed what remained of the Romano-British, Christianized civilization.

In his search for the historical personage of Arthur, Christopher Hibbert brings those troubled times vividly to life. As his intriguing story makes clear, the actual facts about Arthur are very few and more than a little obscure. But enough is known to build a convincing picture of the sixth-century British warrior who was to become a legend all over the world. The speed with which this legend spread and the astonishing richness of the material that embellished such meager historical facts are themselves tributes to Arthur's power to rally brave men to his cause.

Recent years have seen renewed interest in Arthur, both because of the musical Camelot, which has retold the legend in terms of our modern human experience, and because of the archaeological excavations that currently are taking place at South Cadbury Castle in Somerset, England—a site identified with Arthur's Camelot since the sixteenth century. Mr. Hibbert describes the work undertaken there, which has disclosed that the ancient

British hill fort was indeed reoccupied around the beginning of the sixth century–the period in which we believe Arthur to have lived. The most recent reports reveal that excavators there have traced the outlines of a sixth-century feasting hall, which they hope may yet be proved to have been used by Arthur and his warriors.

THE EDITORS

I

Legends and Legacies

In the heart of the quiet, gentle countryside of southwest England is a yellow limestone hill. It rises suddenly and sharply five hundred feet above the little village of South Cadbury, and old men who have lived all their lives in its shadow have strange tales to tell. South Cadbury Castle is a hollow hill, so they say, and if on St. John's Eve you could find the golden gates that lead inside it, there you would discover King Arthur sitting in the middle of his court. Some times on rough winter nights you can hear the king trot by with his hounds along the well-worn track, for, as one old man put it, "folks do say that on the night of the full moon King Arthur and his men ride round the hill, and their horses are shod with silver and a silver shoe has been found in the track where they do ride, and when they have ridden round the hill, they stop to water their horses at the Wishing Well."

For countless generations such legends have been told of Arthur, the "Once and Future King," and of his noble knights. Not only at South Cadbury, which has long been identified with Arthur's palace of Camelot, but all over England, Wales, and Scotland as well, his fame survives in strange myths of unknown antiquity.

Each county has its own legends. In Cornwall the tale goes that all the farmlands and the forests "swarmed with giants until Arthur, the good king, vanished them all with his cross-sword." In Northumberland, beneath the castle of Sewingshields, Arthur and his queen, Guinevere, their knights and their ladies, and the king's pack of hounds all lie sleeping in the vaults. So, too, do they sleep beneath the ruins of Richmond Castle in Yorkshire, waiting to be wakened by the blast of a horn that lies on a table by the entrance to their cavern. An unwary farmer once stumbled across them, it is said, but lacked the courage to blow the horn that would bring them back to life. Wales is full of tales of caves and hollow hills in which Arthur and his knights await the call to return. One day, all these legends agree, King Arthur will be roused from his long slumber and ride forth to save his people, at a time when they most need him.

As well as the legends, there are place names. Arthur, it seems, traveled far and wide, for his name can be found the length and breadth of the country—from the Sdilly islands of Great and Little Arthur off the southwestern coast of Cornwall, to Arthur's Seat, looming above Scotland's capital city of Edinburgh, far to the north; and from Arthur's Chair high in the hills of Breconshire in Wales to Arthur's Hill at Newcastle, on the northeastern coast of Northumberland. No other name in the whole of Britain turns up so frequently, in fact—except that of the Devil. No one knows exactly how old most of these place names are, just as no one knows how old the legends are. But somewhere in the dark mists of history beyond the time of their creation there was a real Arthur who inspired them.

The Arthur who has become part of the fabric of our lives today is mostly a creation of medieval times, when troubadours and chroniclers made him into a hero of romance, a Christian champion, a noble ruler whose knights were patterns of chivalry. These Arthurian tales have taken their place in our literature, and over the centuries poets and painters have created the characters and their adventures anew. The myth has become so real to us, in fact, that we tend to forget the existence of an actual, historical Arthur. He may not have been a king in the sense we understand kingship. He may not have been even a particularly good or generous or idealistic man. All we know, in starting out to search for him, is that he must have been a remarkable person, because fame does not come without good reason, and Arthur's fame never has been equaled.

The earliest known reference to a historical Arthur is an indirect one, dating from the turbulent centuries immediately after A.D. 410, when the last Roman garrison was withdrawn from Britain, the westernmost outpost of a Roman Empire that was crumbling into decay. Following the legions' departures, the island suffered constant invasions by Jutes, Angles, and Saxons from across the North Sea. And in an epic poem written about 603, the Welsh bard, Aneurin describes one of the many battles that took place between these invaders and the Britons, fighting desperately to repel them. From this long poem, *Gododdin*, it appears that Arthur's name already was identified with outstanding courage, for Aneurin describes the feats of a certain British hero by saying that his valor was remarkable, "although he was no Arthur."

Another significant clue is this: A century before *Gododdin* was written, the name Arthur was virtually unknown in Britain. By the late sixth and early seventh centuries, however, it had become fairly common, for there are four or five Arthurs to be traced even in the scanty records that have come down to us from this period. One of them was a prince of Argyll, who was born to the Scottish king, Aedán mac Gabrain about 570; another Arthur was born at much the same time in southwestern Wales, great-grandson of a ruler named Vortiporius, to whom a monument still exists; while in 620 the Irish king, Morgan was killed by one "Artuir, son of Bicoir, a Briton." It is difficult to account for this sudden popularity of the name unless a real Arthur existed at this time, or shortly before, whose exploits had so excited the admiration of his contemporaries that several British leaders named their sons in his honor.

Yet, although these references strongly suggest that a historical Arthur was living in Britain some time during the sixth century, the sources from that period do not mention his name directly. It is not until some two hundred fifty years later, in fact, that Arthur's name first appears in an authentic chronicle: the *Historia*

Brittonum, which was compiled in Latin by a Welsh monk named Nennius in the ninth century. In a series of tantalizingly brief references, Nennius mentions Arthur as the British victor in a series of sixth-century battles fought by the Britons against the Saxons. Nennius gives very little solid information, as we shall see in a later chapter, but he does confirm Arthur's legendary reputation for bravery, suggested by the allusion in the poem *Gododdin*; more importantly, he makes clear that Arthur was a figure around whom fantastic legends already had begun to cluster.

Nennius recounts two stories that illustrate this; justly, he calls them *mirabilia*–marvels. The first concerns Cam Cabal, a cairn, or monument, made from stones piled on top of each other, in the Welsh county of Breconshire. On the top of the cairn was a stone bearing the footprint of Arthur's dog, Cabal, who had so marked it by treading on it during a boar hunt. Arthur had caused the cairn to be built as a memorial to his beloved dog; and whenever the stone with the footprint was removed, unfailingly within twenty-four hours it would be back again on its heap.

The other story was of the miraculous tomb of Arthur's son, Anir, who was buried beside the source of the River Gamber in Herefordshire on the Welsh border. Anir "was the son of Arthur the soldier," Nennius writes, "and Arthur himself killed him there and buried him. And when men come to measure the length of the mound, they find it sometimes six feet, sometimes nine, sometimes twelve, and sometimes fifteen. Whatever length you find it at one time, you will find it different at another, and I myself have proved this to be true."

Fanciful as Nennius' stories may appear, they were far outdone in the early twelfth century, when a scholar known as Geoffrey of Monmouth wrote a book called *Historia Regum Britanniae* (*A History of the Kings of Britain*). In it he gave himself the task of providing an account of "the kings who dwelt in Britain before the coming of Christ," and "especially of King Arthur and the many others who succeeded him after the coming of Christ." Geoffrey probably was born in Monmouth, in South Wales, although he may originally have been of Breton stock; all we know of his parentage for certain is that his father, interestingly enough, was called Arthur. He ended his life as bishop of St. Asaph, a town in North Wales. Twelfth-century Wales and Brittany both were areas where most of the inhabitants were of Celtic origin, which means that they were descended from the original Britons who peopled the Island in Roman times. Geoffrey was an imaginative man who was proud of his origins; he also was a well-read and ambitious man who shared the heritage of the Normans who were Britain's overlords at the time. His *History of the Kings of Britain* combines these influences; thanks to Geoffrey's ability as a writer, it presents the Arthurian legend in a way that appealed to a far wider audience than the Norman noblemen to whom it was dedicated.

The *History* is divided into twelve books, three of which are devoted to King Arthur, and it is quite clear from reading the work that it is he who excites the author's imagination above all the other British kings. Here, for the first time in a written work, Arthur appears as the great romantic hero of Celtic tradition, with a splendid court, a magical sword, a shield painted with the likeness of the Blessed Mary, Mother of God, a spear "thirsty for slaughter," and a helmet whose crest is "carved in the shape of a dragon." His court is as magnificent and as well conducted as that of the Emperor Charlemagne, and its atmosphere is pervaded with twelfth-century chivalric ideals. "For none was thought worthy of a lady's love, unless he had been three times approved in the bearing of arms. And so the ladies were made chaste and the knights the better by their loves."

Here, in Geoffrey's *History of the Kings of Britain* the main traditions of the Arthurian epic are established for the first time, and the stories first told that subsequently would become so well-known. Here, too, is the first appearance of the legend that Arthur did not merely defeat the Saxons, but led British armies overseas on triumphant campaigns that ranged from Ireland to the borders of Italy, bringing them victories worthy of those won by Caesar himself.

According to Geoffrey of Monmouth, his wonderful–or as many were to say, incredible–narrative was based upon "a very ancient book in the British tongue." This had been brought to England from Wales by his friend Walter, Archdeacon of Oxford, "a man well informed about the history of foreign countries, and most learned in all branches of history." Because no one at the time–other than Geoffrey and Walter–appears ever to have seen this ancient book and no Welsh or Breton chronicle that in the least resembles it ever has been discovered, it has long been supposed that Geoffrey simply invented it. Certainly, it was customary in those days, when compiling a history whose accuracy might be questioned, to claim that its authority was vouched for by a learned work of great antiquity. In any case, Geoffrey of Monmouth ended his book with the note that he has left the work of retelling the biographies of the later Welsh and Saxon kings to three other historians who were his contemporaries. Perhaps he expected them also to be his critics, because he recommends that they "say nothing at all about the kings of the Britons, since they have not in their possession the book in the British language which Walter, Archdeacon of Oxford, brought from Wales. It is this book which I have been at such pains to translate thus into Latin, for it was composed very accurately about the deeds of these princes and to their honor."

One historian undeterred by this warning was William of Newburgh, who was born about 1136, the year Geoffrey finished his History, and himself subsequently wrote a history of English affairs from the Norman Conquest onward. A far more critical historian than Geoffrey, William strongly condemned his predecessor's work as fanciful, remarking that if the events it related ever happened, they must have taken place in a different world. Geoffrey, according to William, had made "the little finger of his Arthur thicker than the loins of Alexander the Great." Similarly, another chronicler, writing in the fourteenth century, wondered how it could have come about that Arthur's conquest of thirty kingdoms and his assault upon a Roman emperor should have been overlooked by all Continental historians.

Later historians generally have agreed with these early skeptics in disbelieving the tale about the ancient book found in Wales by the Archdeacon of Oxford. They supposed that Geoffrey based his stories not so much on Nennius' *Historia Brittonum* or on any such recognized authority on early British history, nor even so much on confused national and local traditions, as on his own colorful imagination. It has been noted that Geoffrey's *History* appeared in the troubled reign of King Stephen when the Norman dynasty that ruled England was in danger of losing its power and influence. Its members felt the need for a distinguished and glorious predecessor on the throne. Charlemagne, the precursor and inspiration of the kings of France and Germany, already was an accepted folk hero who, legend said, was not dead but only sleeping, waiting to return in triumph with his paladins. A relationship with the legendary Arthur could greatly benefit the Norman kings in their efforts to throw off French domination.

Other historians have stressed the fact that Geoffrey of Monmouth was brought up in Wales and in the atmosphere of Celtic lore and that while flattering the royal court by presenting Arthur as the ideal of an Anglo-Norman king, he also was flattering the Celts by exaggerating the splendors of their own past. In fact, he 'was not really writing history at all, but a tract that would demonstrate the heroic virtues of the British race and their leaders by recounting their stupendous victories over all their enemies.

Yet, Geoffrey of Monmouth occupies a very important place in this story. For it was he who first created an Arthurian legend that fired the imagination of the whole of Christendom. In his own country, his success was immediate. The enormous popularity of his work can be judged from the fact that nearly two hundred full manuscripts of it have survived, some fifty of which actually date from the twelfth century. Throughout the Middle Ages Geoffrey's *History* remained the primary source for all writers about Celtic Britain.

But it was on the Continent that the legend was most widely expanded and embellished. As early as the 1140's, Geoffrey Gaimar had translated Geoffrey's *History* from Latin into French; and in 1155 the Anglo-Norman poet Maistre Wace brought out a verse paraphrase, *Le Roman de Brut* (named for a totally mythical Brutus of Troy who, in Geoffrey's account, was the founder of Britain). This makes the story even more dramatic and romantic, introducing the legend of the Round Table, around which Arthur's knights sit in feast and conference, and presenting Arthur as "a lover of glory, whose famous deeds are right fit to be kept in remembrance: he ordained the courtesies of courts, and observed high state in a very splendid fashion."

Around 1175, the Arthurian legend was taken up by the French poet Chrétien de Troyes. A skillful compiler of romances for the French feudal aristocracy, Chrétien added to the stories fresh characters and a fresh flavor, casting the tales in a strangely unreal, ethereal setting in which love was a kind of religion. In this he was responding to the wishes of his patroness, Countess Marie de Champagne, whose brilliant court was the center for this new code of courtly love. It glorified an ideal kind of affection between a knight and his lady—who could not be his wife, since all marriages were "arranged" in those days and true love within a relationship of duty was out of the question. The ideals of courtly love were that the lover should be humble and courteous and revere and obey his lady almost as if she were his lord. In return, the lady would reward his devotion by loving him as completely as she cared to. Understandably, the ideals of courtly love became extremely popular and the stories that glorified it were read and recited all over Europe.

Following Chrétien's example, several other French writers produced prose and verse romances, some largely imitative, others containing an altered version of an old story or a freshly interpolated tale, and began grouping them together. Storytellers from Brittany almost certainly added to the increasing body of material with their detailed accounts of Arthurian adventures, based on the old Celtic tales of marvels and magic, which they retold as they wandered from one nobleman's hall to the next.

Meanwhile, in England, a Worcestershire priest named Layamon translated Wace's *Roman de Brut* from French into English, once again expanding and elaborating the basic material. In Layamon's *Brut*, the first version of the Arthurian legend to be written in English, the emphasis changes once more: Layamon was writing not for the aristocracy, whose language was still French, but for the common people of England, who spoke an antique form of the language that we ourselves use and were interested chiefly in the characters and adventures already familiar to them from their native heritage. Layamon treats the legend as an epic of early Britain in which Arthur is a practical, nationalistic, somewhat barbaric leader, very different from the kind of magical fairy king who appears in the French romances. This earthier, more straightforward Arthur is an essentially British hero, and this treatment of him is carried on in several later poems and prose romances written in English that retell the adventures of the king and his knights.

Strangely enough, the first appearance of King Arthur in a work of art now extant was not in his native, realm of Britain, but in Italy, far to the south, where a relief of Arthur and his knights was carved above the north doorway of Modena Cathedral some time between 1099 and 1120. In 1165, Arturus Rex again was depicted, this time on a mosaic pavement in the cathedral of Otranto, on the southern heel of Italy. The mosaic portrays the king bearing a scepter and riding a goat, which seems a rather odd mount for a king, except that goats at that time had some association with those who ruled subterranean kingdoms, as Arthur was supposed to do.

About thirty years after this pavement was laid down, an English visitor to the island of Sicily, not far distant, reported that its inhabitants believed that King Arthur could be found in the volcanic depths below Mount Etna. He also had been seen on a Sicilian plain by a groom in search of a runaway horse. This man had crossed the plain, entered a marvelous palace, and there had found King Arthur lying on a bed. The king told him of his last battle and that each year, on the anniversary of that battle, his wounds broke out afresh. It seems surprising that the tradition of Arthur's survival should have traveled so far from its British origins, but the island of Sicily was ruled at this time by a Norman dynasty and the legend could well have been imported by storytellers in their service and instantly transplanted into a Mediterranean setting by their eager listeners.

Within two centuries the legend of King Arthur and his knights had spread all over Europe and even into parts of Asia. In France Arthur's fame almost eclipsed that of Charlemagne, who was not restored to his former pre-eminent position until after the Middle Ages had drawn to a close. In Germany the finest medieval poets celebrated Arthur's great deeds and the adventures of his knights, particularly Tristram and Percival. In Italy Dante wrote of Lancelot. From Ireland to Greece there were translations of Arthurian texts. His was a familiar name throughout the Low Countries, in Scandinavia and Switzerland, Spain and Portugal, Cyprus and Sicily.

"Whither has not flying fame spread the name of Arthur the Briton?" asked an English writer as early as the 1170's. "Even as far as the empire of Christendom extends. Who, I say, does not speak of Arthur the Briton, since he is almost better known to the people of Asia than to the

Britanni, as our pilgrims returning from the East inform us. The Eastern people speak of him, as do the Western, though separated by the width of the whole earth."

Early in the thirteenth century noblemen and knights began amusing themselves with festivities that came to be called Round Tables, in honor of the great table around which Arthur's knights had sat at Camelot. The idea of a round table that would make no distinction between the ranks of the knights who sat at it seemed to have a particular appeal to the medieval mind, no doubt in contrast to the strict rules of precedence that governed every other activity, especially eating in company. Crusaders who baffled in earnest to free the Holy Land from Moslem domination also disported themselves with jousts and banquets that honored the legendary King Arthur; the lord of Beirut honored the knighting of his eldest sons with a splendid celebration at which "there was much giving and spending; there were *bohorts* [a kind of tourney at which blunted weapons were used], the adventures of Britain and the Round Table were enacted, and there were many other amusements."

Similar Round Table festivities are reported from places as diverse as the island of Cyprus in 1223, Acre in the Holy Land in 1286, Valencia in Spain in 1269, Prague in 1319, and as far west as Dublin in 1498. At these and many other places, kings, dukes, and emperors presided at Round Tables and founded orders in imitation of King Arthur's "goodly fellowship." They, their knights, guests, and rivals adopted the names, supposed heraldic badges, splendid clothes, and equipages of Arthur's famous knights and competed in energetic and dangerous tournaments for the pleasure or the favors of the ladies of the court.

Pope after pope condemned the extravagances of the Round Tables, their immorality, their wantonness and danger; those who died after a particularly heavy fall or ferocious buffet were denied Christian burial. Yet the Round Table continued to be the most fashionable of all diversions among the nobility of Europe.

Although principally associated with the aristocracy, the Round Table was not an exclusively upper-class activity. In 1281, a citizen of Magdeburg in Saxony sent out invitations to various merchants of his acquaintance asking them to attend a Round Table and try their prowess, the proved champion to be awarded the prize of a woman named Dame Feie. Those who came to show their skill were met by constables outside the city and escorted to the lists, or tourney ground, which had been set up in marshy ground not far away. The shields of the defending champions were hung from trees, and a touch with a lance-point on one would bring its owner out from his tent nearby to meet the challenger and defend his honor in the lists. Dame Feie was indeed won by an old merchant who presented her with a rich dowry but it is hard to believe that he won her by force of arms alone.

One of the most magnificent of all medieval tournaments was held at Windsor Castle in 1344. Edward III ordered it to celebrate two resounding victories against England's traditional enemies, France and Scotland, and after three days of jousting and feasting, the King called a solemn assembly of all his guests. Dressed in velvet robes and wearing the crown of England, he placed his hand on the Bible and "took a corporeal oath that he would begin a Round Table in the same manner and condition as the Lord Arthur, formerly King of England, appointed it, namely to the number of 300 knights,...and he would cherish it and maintain it according to his power." Edward selected his knights, binding them to himself, to one another, and to the service of the weak and oppressed, with solemn oaths; and then, says the chronicler, the kettle drums and trumpets sounded "all together, and the guests hastened to a feast; which feast was complete with richness of fare, variety of dishes, and overflowing abundance of drinks; the delight was unutterable, the comfort inestimable, the enjoyment unalloyed, the hilarity without care."

A few days later, in the huge courtyard of the castle's Upper Ward, work began on the building of a great stone hall for the Round Table, where the knights of the fellowship could in future hold their feasts. Soon afterward, it had to be suspended, for the King went to war with France once more and could not afford the double expense. He returned to Windsor in 1347, triumphant after his crushing victory over the French at Crécy and his capture of the port of Calais, the key to the English Channel. The unfinished hall for the knights of the Round Table still stood in the Upper Ward to remind him of his intentions. Edward was a man of great ambition, who took his obligations as a knight and as a leader of knights more seriously than his responsibility as sovereign. Pleasure and feasting occupied him only for a while. Soon he was considering an enterprise "more particular and more select," the revival of his idea for a fellowship of knights that would be the envy of Europe.

So it was that the Round Table of King Arthur became the original inspiration of the

Order of the Garter. This order, which took its name from the badges worn by the knights who competed in a tournament held at Windsor in 1348, was to become, and still remains, in the twentieth century, the most noble and respected order of knighthood in Europe.

By the time the order was founded, however, the ideas of chivalry already were dying. Battles were no longer to be won by sheer bravery, by knights fighting each other with sword and lance. Edward III's own victory at Crécy had proved that a quantity of low-born English longbow-men, posted advantageously, could gain a victory over a knightly army twice the size, despite its superior armor and aristocratic birth. At Agincourt, in 1415, the lesson was hammered home still more strongly when a French army fifty-thousand strong clashed with an English force of thirteen thousand. Thousands of French knights, the glory of the chivalry of King Charles VI, disdained to allow a place in the front line to inferior troops and the new and despised artillery. Dismounted, in a dense metal wedge, unable to move in the muddy fields, they were at the mercy of the English archers and men-at-arms. The Englishmen, with freedom to maneuver, simply tumbled the French knights to the ground in their heavy, suffocating armor and chopped them to pieces with their own swords and battle-axes.

Within another half-century, England itself was to be torn asunder by civil war as the brutal Wars of the Roses convulsed the country. The Middle Ages were drawing to a close; new ideas, new ways of life, new inventions were being introduced. In 1476 William Caxton set up the first printing press in England and began to print for a growing audience books that previously had been available only in laboriously copied manuscript: Chaucer's *Canterbury Tales*, translations from the classics, an encyclopaedia of philosophy.

On July 31, 1485, Caxton published his sixty-second title from the sign of the Red Pale in the London parish of Westminster. Within a month, the first Tudor king of England would ascend the throne; a new era, a Tudor era, was about to begin. Yet the book Caxton printed that July was the most renowned of all medieval romances, Sir Thomas Malory's *Le Morte d'Arthur*—a book that looked back with a kind of nostalgic longing to the glories and heroic achievements of a more chivalrous age, to a strange, past world, already forgotten and idealized.

2

A "Noble and Joyous Book"

Caxton called it a "noble and joyous book," and so it is. But *Le Morte d'Arthur* is far more than that. It is full of a strange sense of doom that foreshadows the "dolorous death and departing out of this world" of its great hero and his valiant knights. Its author was a prisoner when he wrote it, a prisoner who longed for the day of his deliverance—and that is almost all that we know of him. He probably was Sir Thomas Malory, a Warwickshire gentleman who at one time served as Member of Parliament for his county. Later, however, he apparently turned to a life of crime. A long series of accusations of rape, robbery, cattle thieving, extortion of money by threats, and attempted murder are recorded against him, and he certainly was imprisoned for some years in Newgate jail in London. It seems strange that such a lawless character should be the author of a book full of knightly adventures and noble deeds. But in the troubled times of the Wars of the Roses, many men spent long years in prison, and the fact that Malory was accused of these crimes does not necessarily mean that he was guilty of them. There is no record of a trial or of sentence being passed upon him.

Some historians, however, prefer to believe that *Le Morte d 'Arthur* was written by a Thomas Malory of Studley and Hutton in Yorkshire while he was a prisoner-of-war in France. It also is possible that its author was neither of these men but yet another Thomas Malory, whose identity remains to be discovered. All that can be said with certainty is that in *Le Morte d' Arthur* he wrote a masterpiece, the one and only medieval romance that has retained its hold on the imagination of five centuries of readers, right down to the present day. Skillfully, painstakingly, the prisoner-knight labored to gather its threads together from the countless existing Arthurian romances—Some French, some English, some in verse, some in prose; and this is the story that he told:

In the days when Uther Pendragon was king of all England, there lived in Cornwall a mighty duke, the Duke of Tintagel, who had a most beautiful wife named Igrayne. The king fell in love with Igrayne, and one day when she was a guest in the royal palace, he took her aside and asked her to sleep with him. But Igrayne was good as well as beautiful and she refused him. Then she told her husband what the king had proposed and begged him to take her from the palace that very night and to ride with her through the darkness to their own castle.

They secretly departed; and when they had gone, the king, in his great anger and burning desire for Igrayne, fell sick. His knights believed that only one man could cure him of his distress, and that was the wizard Merlin. Merlin was sent for, and when he came to the king, he announced that he could, indeed, make him better and that he even could arrange for him to make love to Igrayne; but there was one condition: "The first night that you shall lie by Igrayne you shall get a child on her; and when that child is born, then you must deliver it to me for me to nourish and look after."

The king agreed; and then Merlin said to him, "Now make you ready. This night you shall lie with Igrayne in the castle of Tintagel, and you shall be made by magic to look like the duke, her husband." Thus, in the guise of the duke, the king rode to Tintagel and was welcomed by Igrayne to her bed. In due time the baby was born, as Merlin had foretold, and in accordance with the promise King Uther had made, the child was wrapped in cloth of gold and handed over to the care of the wizard. Merlin, in turn, entrusted him to Sir Ector, a true and honest knight and the lord of fine estates in England and Wales. Sir Ector's wife fed him at her breast; and they called a priest to christen him, and the name they gave him was Arthur.

The years passed, King Uther died, and England stood in danger of civil war because the great barons could not agree on who should succeed him. On Merlin's advice, the Archbishop of Canterbury sent for all the quarreling lords and gentlemen-at-arms to come to London at Christmas time and pray to Jesus to show them by some miracle who had the best right to be king. The lords and gentlemen came to London and went to the greatest church there before day break to pray and hear Mass. After they had knelt down, there suddenly appeared in the churchyard a big square marble stone. In the stone was fixed a blacksmith's anvil; in the anvil was a great sword, with its point imbedded in the steel; and around the sword was written in letters of gold:

WHOSO PULLETH OUT THIS SWORD OF THIS
STONE AND ANVIL IS RIGHTWISE KING BORN
OF ALL ENGLAND

Then all the people marveled; but not one of
the lords who struggled with all their power to
pull the sword from the anvil could move it so
much as the fraction of an inch.

"The man who can pluck out the sword is
not here," the Archbishop pronounced. "But do
not doubt that God will make him known."

Now it had been arranged that on New Year's
Day the lords and knights should ride into the
fields outside the city to compete in a tournament; and it happened that two of the knights
attending the tournament were the good Sir
Ector and his son Kay, who had been knighted
recently and was eager to prove his valor. With
them was Kay's young foster brother, Arthur,
acting as his squire. As they were riding to the
tourney ground, Sir Kay suddenly realized that
he foolishly had left his sword behind in his
father's London lodgings, and he sent Arthur
galloping back to fetch it for him. But when
Arthur reached town, he found that the door
of the lodgings was locked, for all the servants
had left to see the tournament. Then Arthur said
to himself, "I will ride to the churchyard and

take the sword with me that sticks in the stone;
for my brother, Sir Kay, shall not be without a
sword this day."

As Malory tells it:

So whan he cam to the chircheyard, sir Arthur alight and
tayed his hors to the style, and so he wente to the tente
and found no knyghtes there, for they were atte justyng.
And so he handled the swerd by the handels, and lightly
and fiersly pulled it out of the stone, and took his hors
and rode his way untyll he came to his broder sir Kay and
delyverd hym the swerd.

As soon as he saw the sword, Sir Ector understood the marvelous thing that Arthur had
done, and immediately he rode with him
back to London, where he told him to place
the sword back in the anvil and pull it out
again. Arthur did so; and although all the lords
thereafter tried to do as he did, none could
move the sword but Arthur. Whereupon all
the people cried out with one voice, "We will
have Arthur for our king. We will have no more
delay. It is God's will that he shall be our king,
and we will kill any man who holds against
it."

Then they all knelt down before him, rich
and poor alike. Malory goes on:

> And Arthur foryaf [forgave] hem and took the swerd bit-
> wene both his handes and offred it upon the aulter where
> the Archebisshop was, and so was he made knyghte of [by]
> the best man that was there. And so anon was the coro-
> nacyon made, and ther was he sworne unto his lordes and
> the comyns [common people] for to be a true kyng, to
> stand with true justyce fro thens forth the dayes of this
> lyf.★

Now that he was king of England, Arthur set out at the head of his knights to fight against all the evil barons who were oppressing his people and against all the rebel lords who would not accept his right to the crown. Among these rebel lords was King Lot of Lo hian and Orkney, who scornfully refused to recognize as king, a beard-less boy who was not even of royal blood. While Arthur was at war in Wales, King Lot's wife, Morgause, came to his headquarters in the city of Caerleon, pretending to bring him a message, but really to spy upon him.

Now, this Queen Morgause was the daughter of Igrayne and the Duke of Tintagel, and thus

---

★ These extracts are taken from the most recent and most authentic edition of works, edited by Professor Eugène Vinaver and published by the Oxford University Press, on which this whole chapter is based. For easier reading, however, we have retold subsequent quotations in modern English.

she was Arthur's half-sister. But Arthur did not know this, and when Morgause came to him with her four young sons, Gawain, Gaheris, Agravaine, and Gareth, she was so beautiful, so richly dressed, and so desirable, that Arthur "cast great love unto her and desired to lie by her." And so they were agreed, and he begat upon his sister a child, and the name of the child was Mordred.

One day, soon after this, King Arthur was riding with Merlin beside a lake. He had broken his sword in all the fighting he had done, but Merlin told him not to worry—"hereby is a sword that shall be yours if I can." Then Arthur noticed, in the middle of the lake, an arm appearing out of the water and in its hand was a shining sword. Catching sight of a young woman walking by the lake, he said to her, "Damsel, what sword is that yonder that the arm holds above the water? I would it were mine, for I have no sword."

"Sir Arthur," replied the damsel, "that sword is mine and you shall have it. Go into yonder barge and row yourself to the sword and take it and the scabbard with you." All of which Arthur did accordingly; and he called the sword, Excalibur, which means "cut steel."

Armed with Excalibur, King Arthur sailed across the Channel to fight the Roman Emperor Lucius, who had demanded a tribute that the

English were not prepared to pay. On his way he stopped to save the people of Normandy from the giant of Mont-St.-Michel, whom he found gnawing on the roasted limbs of newborn babies. "There was never devil in hell more horriblier made" than this giant, who was thirty feet tall and the foulest sight that ever man saw. He snatched up an iron club and swiped at Arthur so hard that his crown fell off. But Arthur fearlessly grappled with him, "and so they weltered and tumbled over the crags and bushes" until they finally rolled right down the mount to the seashore. And there, Arthur plunged a dagger into the giant's ribs and killed him.

Then Arthur marched south into the province of Champagne, and in a great baffle there he overwhelmed the Emperor Lucius and killed him with his own hands. With his army, he traveled onward over the mountains into Italy, overcoming all his enemies, Saracens, and monsters as he marched, and was himself crowned emperor in Rome by the Pope. On his return to England he was met by all his court, who escorted him in triumph to Camelot.

King Arthur's knights had long been pressing him to take a wife. When the king sought Merlin's advice, the magician asked him if there was any woman he loved more than another.

"Yea," said King Arthur, "I love Guinevere,

43

daughter of King Leodegrance of Cameliard who holds in his house the Round Table that was given to him by my father, King Uther; and Guinevere is the fairest damsel that I know or could ever find." But Merlin, who had the gift of seeing into the future, warned Arthur against Guinevere. He insisted that she would not be faithful to her husband but would fall in love with his noblest knight, and that this noblest knight, Sir Lancelot, would fall in love with her. Yet Arthur paid no attention; he was determined to take Guinevere for his wife, whatever Merlin said. Therefore, Merlin went to King Leodegrance of Cameliard to tell him of Arthur's desire.

"That is the best tidings that ever I heard," said King Leodegrance, who esteemed Arthur as a most noble and worthy king. "I shall send him a gift that shall please him, for I shall give him the Round Table which Uther, his father, gave me. There are places at it for a hundred and fifty knights, and I shall fill a hundred of those places myself by sending him a hundred good knights."

"Now, Merlin," said King Arthur when he heard this news, "go and find me fifty knights of the most courage and renown in all this land." And Merlin went forth, but he brought only twenty-eight knights back to Camelot because he could find no more who were worthy to sit at the Round Table. One of them was Arthur's nephew Gawain, who was to be knighted on the day of the wedding. And Guinevere and King Arthur were married in the church of St. Stephen at Camelot with great solemnity.

Then the Archbishop of Canterbury was fetched to bless the seats of the Round Table while all the knights were in their places; and after they had risen and gone to pay homage to King Arthur, there was found in every seat, in letters of gold, the name of the knight to whom the place belonged, or would belong, save for two seats, which had no names at all. And Merlin told the king that no knight should sit in those places but those who were the worthiest of all. Each knight was given riches and land and was charged by King Arthur never to commit murder or robbery or do any evil thing, always to grant mercy to those who asked for mercy, and upon pain of death, to go to the help of ladies in distress.

All the knights promised to obey these laws, and all of them were brave and noble men; yet one of them stood out above all the others in nobility and courage, and this was Sir Lancelot of the Lake, son of the king of Benwick. As Merlin had foretold, he performed many chivalrous deeds for Queen Guinevere, "whom he loved above all other ladies all the days of his life." And the queen fell in love with him.

But King Arthur did not know of their love; and he and Sir Lancelot and Sir Lancelot's son, Sir Galahad, and Sir Tristram, Sir Gawain, Sir Gareth, Sir Percival, Sir Bors, and Sir Bedivere and all the other members of the noble fellow ship went out upon many adventures and quests. They sought to slay the monstrous Questing Beast; they laid siege to castles; they took part in dangerous battles and exciting tournaments; they strove to gain the love of fair ladies; above all, they endeavored to find the Holy Grail, the holy vessel that Christ Himself used at the Last Supper. It suddenly and mysteriously had appeared one evening at Camelot, covered with rich white silk, and after filling the hall where the king and his knights sat with brilliant light and sweet perfumes, it was borne away suddenly no one knew where. Nearly all the knights joined in the quest for the Holy Grail, to the sorrow both of King Arthur, who feared that they would never afterward return to the Round Table, and of Queen Guinevere, who grieved to see them—and in particular, Sir Lancelot—depart from Camelot. Yet although Sir Lancelot tried with all his strength of body and mind, although he did penances, humbled himself, and wore a hair shirt for more than a year, he never could do more than glimpse the Holy Grail from far off, for no knight could complete the quest who was, not completely free from sin. Only Sir Galahad, Sir Percival, and Sir Bors were pure enough to be worthy; and after they had successfully found the Grail and mystically achieved the quest, the sacred vessel was borne up to heaven and never seen again.

However hard Sir Lancelot had tried to live honorably and forget his passion for the queen, he found that he could not banish her from his thoughts. Soon after his return from the Grail quest, they were meeting secretly once more. "So they loved together more hotter than they did before and had many such secret trysts together that many in the court of Camelot spoke of it." Loudest in their talk against the queen and Lancelot were Sir Gawain's brother Sir Agravaine and his half-brother, Sir Mordred, the king's son. One day in the king's chamber Sir Agravaine said openly, "I marvel that we all be not ashamed both to see and to know how Sir Lancelot lies daily and nightly by the queen. Fall whatsoever fall may, I will disclose it to the king."

True to his threat, Sir Agravaine, accompanied by Sir Mordred, went to the king and told him what people were whispering about the queen and Sir Lancelot, and he urged him to set a trap to catch them out. "My lord," said Sir Agravaine, "you shall ride to-morrow a-hunting, and doubt you not, Lancelot will not go with you. And so when it draws toward night, send word to the queen that you will stay out all night, and send for your cooks. And then upon pain of death that night we shall take him with the queen, and we shall bring him to you, alive or dead."

King Arthur was loath to believe them, for he dearly loved both his wife and Sir Lancelot. But in the end he agreed. The next morning he went out hunting and sent word to the queen that he would be out all night. Sir Agravaine and Sir Mordred and twelve other knights who were jealous of Sir Lancelot hid in a chamber next door to the queen's chamber and waited silently for her lover to join her. Once he was inside the room, his enemies rushed to the door and cried out, "You traitor, Sir Lancelot, now you are taken! Come out of the queen's chamber!"

Sir Lancelot had no armor but his sword, but he was determined not to be taken. He wrapped his cloak tightly round his sword arm and called through the door, "Now, fair lords, leave your noise and your rushing, and I shall set open this door and then you may do with me what you like." Then he unbarred the door and opened it a crack so that only one man at a time might get through. The first who came was Sir Colgrevance of Gore, who struck out at Sir Lancelot with all his strength; but Lancelot deflected the blow with his thickly wrapped arm and knocked his opponent groveling to the floor.

"Then Sir Lancelot with great might drew the knight within the chamber door, and with the help of the queen and her ladies was armed in Colgrevance's armor, and set open the chamber door and mightily strode in among the knights. And anon, at the first stroke he slew Sir Agravaine and anon, after, twelve of his fellows, for there was none of the twelve knights might stand Sir Lancelot one buffet. And also he wounded Sir Mordred, and therewithal Mordred fled with all his might…to King Arthur, sore wounded and all bloodied.

"'Ah! Jesu, mercy! How may this be?' said the king. 'Took you him in the queen's chamber?'

"'Yea! So God me help!' said Sir Mordred, 'There we found him.' And so he told the king from the beginning to the ending…

"'Alas,' said the king, 'now I am sure the noble fellowship of the Round Table is broken for ever.'"

Overwhelmed with grief, Arthur gave orders that the queen must be burned to death for treason in accordance with the laws of England.

Sir Gawain pleaded with his uncle not to do so, but Arthur would not listen to him. Gawain refused to be present, and the king commanded his younger brothers, Gareth and Gaheris, to escort the queen to the stake and witness her punishment. They were as reluctant as Sir Gawain, but too young to disobey the king's command. In token of their protest, however, they insisted on attending the queen to her execution unarmed.

Guinevere was led to the stake, outside the city of Carlisle, and a priest heard her last confession. But just as the fire was about to be lit, Sir Lancelot and a large band of his friends galloped up, wildly lashing out with their swords, and striking to the ground all those who resisted them. "And in this rushing and hurling, as Sir Lancelot pressed hither and thither, it misfortuned him to slay Sir Gaheris and Sir Gareth," whom he did not recognize in the confusion. Then Lancelot cut Guinevere loose from her bonds and rode away with her to his castle, Joyous Garde, where his friends flocked to join him.

When news was brought to Arthur of this affray, and of the death of Gaheris and Gareth, the king fainted from pure sorrow. When he came to, he began to bewail the loss of "the fairest fellowship of noble knights that Christian king ever held together. Within these two days I have lost nigh forty knights and also the noble fellowship of Sir Lancelot and his blood. And the death of Sir Gaheris and Sir Gareth will cause the greatest mortal war that ever was, for I am sure that when their brother, Sir Gawain, knows thereof I shall never have rest of him till I have destroyed Sir Lancelot. And therefore, wit you well, my heart was never so sorry as it is now. And much more am I sorrier for my good knights' loss than for the loss of my fair queen, for queens I might have enough, but such a fellowship of good knights shall never be together again."

King Arthur sent through all England to summon his knights, and then he laid siege to Sir Lancelot in Joyous Garde. There were many battles, but in all of them Sir Lancelot held back and would not fight his hardest, because he loved Arthur and had no heart to fight against him. At last, the Pope interceded to arrange a truce by which Arthur would forgive Guinevere and take her back again. But Sir Gawain would not allow the king to forgive Sir Lancelot. Thus Lancelot was banished to his Kingdom of Benwick in France, and King Arthur and Sir Gawain crossed the Channel with sixty thousand men to make war on him there.

In Arthur's absence Mordred, who had been

appointed regent of England and guardian of
Queen Guinevere, seized his chance to replace
his father on the throne. He pretended that he
had received a letter announcing King Arthur's
death, and with that excuse, he called a parliament and had himself chosen king and crowned
at Canterbury. Then he rode to Winchester and
told Guinevere that since her husband was dead,
he would marry her himself.

But Queen Guinevere fled away to London
and took the Tower of London, "and suddenly
in all haste possible she stuffed it with all manner
of victual, and well garnished it with men, and
so kept it. Then Sir Mordred was passing wroth
out of measure. And a short tale for to make, he
went and laid a mighty siege about the Tower
of London, and made many great assaults, and
threw many great engines unto them and shot
great guns."

When news came that Arthur was returning
home to be avenged, however, Sir Mordred had
to lift the siege and make for Dover to oppose
the landing of his father's troops. At Dover "there
was much slaughter of gentle knights and many
a bold baron was laid full low." But both Arthur
and Mordred survived to fight again another day;
and on that day there was "never seen a more
dolefuller battle in no Christian land." From
morning until night the fighting raged, until a

hundred thousand noble knights lay dead upon the field. "Then was King Arthur wroth out of measure when he saw his people so slain, and he looked about him and was aware where stood Sir Mordred leaning upon his sword among a great heap of dead men."

Gripping his spear in both hands, he ran upon Mordred, crying out, "Traitor! Now is thy death day come!" With all his force he plunged his spear into Mordred's stomach beneath the shield, and its point passed right through Mordred's body and came bursting out of his back. But with his death's wound upon him, Mordred raised his sword and struck his father so ferocious a blow upon the helmet that the steel edge cut through the visor and entered Arthur's skull.

"And noble Arthur fell in a swoon to the earth, and there he swooned oftentimes." Sir Bedivere, the last of his knights still left alive, although he, too, was grievously wounded, knelt down and held the king in his arms.

"My time passes fast, Sir Bedivere," King Arthur said. "Take my good sword, Excalibur, and go with it to yonder water's side and throw it into the water."

Sir Bedivere went to the lake nearby and hurled Excalibur as far across the water as he could; and as it fell, a hand came up to grasp it by the handle, to wave it three times in farewell, before taking it down into the deep. Then Sir Bedivere took the king upon his back and carried him down to the water's edge. Here stood a little barge in which sat many fair ladies wearing black veils and weeping bitterly.

"Now put me into that barge," said King Arthur, "For I must go into the vale of Avalon to heal me of my grievous wound. And if thou hear nevermore of me, pray for my soul." Sir Bedivere had put the king down gently, laying his head upon the lap of one of the ladies, and the barge sailed away into the mists, and King Arthur was heard of no more.

"Yet some men say in many parts of England King Arthur is not dead but had by the will of our Lord Jesus into another place. And men say that he shall come again and he shall win the Holy Cross. And many men say that there is written upon the tomb this:

HIC IACET ARTHURUS, REX QUONDAM
REXQUE FUTURUS
Here lies King Arthur, the Once and Future King

Such is the theme of Malory's story, and such its atmosphere. Based on earlier French romances, which were themselves based on Geoffrey of Monmouth's *History of the Kings of Britain*, which, in turn, was based on who knows what earlier records, legends, and oral traditions, it has taken us a long way from the harsh reality of the fifth century and from the threatened island of Britain in which the real Arthur was born.

3

The Threatened
Islands

The fifth century witnessed the disintegration of the Roman Empire. For years Rome had been striving to defend its farflung frontiers, which stretched some 10,000 miles, from the North Sea along the Rhine and across to the Danube, and so to the shores of the Black Sea; and from Constantinople right around the Mediterranean to the Strait of Gibraltar, then northward through Spain and Gaul–Roman provinces for centuries– to Britain, the island that marked Rome's farthest expansion to the northwest. But the once-civilized Roman way of life had become sterile and decadent; Rome's emperors were men of little importance, puppets in the hands of their generals, who frequently assassinated them and took their places on the throne. The superb administration that had enabled the government in Rome to keep control of an unwieldy conglomeration of nations and provinces had degenerated into a bureaucracy riddled with corruption. Trade declined as taxes increased. The Roman army, once so proud of its legions of well-equipped soldiers, more and more consisted of troops of barbarians, hired to defend the empire against steadily increasing pressure from other bands of barbarians–Goths, Vandals, Saxons, Huns–moving southward and westward from Scandinavia, the lands around the Baltic, and the distant Russian steppes.

In 429, under the leadership of their cunning and ruthless King Gaiseric, a horde of Vandals poured out of Spain and into Roman Africa, the main source of Rome's corn supply and the home of a prosperous civilization. They made their way along the North African coast, conquering and pillaging as they went, and in 439 they captured Carthage, Rome's great African seaport. Gaiseric ordered the building of a great pirate fleet, and using Carthage as their base, the Vandals began to ravage the Roman cities around the Mediterranean Sea and even to threaten Rome itself.

Already endangered by barbarian pressure along its northern and eastern frontiers, Rome no longer could offer any protection to the distant island of Britain. One legion after another was called back to fight Rome's wars on the Continent, until only a small regular garrison remained. By 410, most of that had been withdrawn, and although there may have been a brief decade of reoccupation between 417 and 429, by the middle of the century, Roman power effectively had ended. The islanders were left to fend for themselves.

For almost a century already, Roman Britain had been under intermittent attack. From the north there was constant raiding by fierce, tattooed Pictish tribesmen, who came down from the Caledónian mountains of Scotland. In the second century A.D. the Emperor Hadrian had built a great wall across the country from east to west between the River Tyne and the Solway Firth, to keep the Picts out of the Romanized country farther south. But once the legions that had defended it with their lives were gone, the Picts clambered over the abandoned ramparts and swarmed south toward the Humber. The Picts were followed by the Scotti, marauders from Ireland, who sailed across the Irish Sea in their light skin-and-wood boats called curraghs. They pillaged wherever they landed on the western coasts of England and Wales, terrifying the fishermen and farmers spearing and knifing those who could not escape, and setting fire to their thatched-roof huts. Far worse a threat than either the Picts or the Irish war-bands, however, was the growing power of the Saxons, users of the seax or short-sword, and their northern neighbors the Angles and the Jutes, who fished and farmed in what is now southern Denmark.

The Angles, Jutes, and Saxons were expanding nations that no longer were content with their restricted farmlands on the Continental mainland. As Roman power declined in Britain, they had begun to look west for more land on which to settle, a rich land that had been a Roman province for more than three hundred years, where there would be plenty of plunder and a good life for all. They came across the North Sea in long, shallow-draught galleys roughly constructed of overlapping oak planks, curved up at either end, and rowed by a score of sturdy warriors. They were a fair people with long hair and beards, clothed in thick, coarse shirts and trousers, in cloaks to which skins were sewn by their women so as to give them extra warmth when they were used as blankets at night. As well as their short-swords, they carried thick, iron-spiked spears, battle-axes, and round wooden shields covered with hide. Few of them wore helmets; fewer still wore coats of ring mail, which cost good money from the armorers of the Rhineland. Even among the leaders there were some who did not even have a thick leather jerkin to protect them. But they were ruthless, violent men who exulted in their animal energy, and all along the southern and eastern coasts of Britain they pillaged and looted, raped and murdered, burning the farms, killing the livestock, and then sailing home.

Late-fourth-century Britain was still one of the most pleasant provinces of the western Roman Empire, though no longer so prosperous as it had been. The rolling downs and plains of the south and west were dotted with the stucco-and-brick villas of gentlemen-farmers—although many had been abandoned and now stood empty, their brightly painted walls already crumbling into ruins, and the pinkish tiles beginning to fall from their roofs. In winter, the well-furnished rooms of these villas had been warmed by heated flues that ran beneath their mosaic floors; in summer, fountains used to play in the courtyards and grape vines grew against the garden walls. Outside their gates good, straight roads still led to the towns that had been Rome's chief contribution to the British way of life—towns whose paved streets and imposing buildings were constructed in the regular, rectilinear manner favored by the architects of Rome.

Roads intersected the island, linking northern fortress with southern port, garrison with tribal capital, stretching from the forts along Hadrian's Wall to the clustered villas of the South Downs, from the legionary fortress at Chester in the west to the large town of Caistor-next-Norwich on the east coast. And at the center of this complex of roads stood Londinium, one of the most impressive cities north of the Alps.

Roman London was a city of some 30,000 inhabitants, living in an area of over three hundred acres enclosed by three miles of strong stone walls, nine feet thick, up to twenty feet high, and pierced by gates where the main roads led through them. The river gate, which faced the traveler as he came across the wide wooden bridge spanning the Thames, opened onto the street leading up to the Basilica, which was the center of commerce and government, a vast and impressive building, more than 420 feet long, with high arcaded walls. Just inside this river gate were the public baths, and other bathhouses were dotted all over the city. Down the streets on either side as far as the eye could see were the wide, arched fronts of the numerous shops and countinghouses and the porticoed homes of the prosperous merchants.

Life in Londinium, like life in the other big towns of Roman Britain, was well organized and pleasant for all but the poor and the slaves who did the heavy work. The farms outside the walls, and the gardens within them, produced fine meat, vegetables, and fruit; fresh, clear water, piped in hollowed tree trunks, was plentiful; the Thames, at whose wharves were moored scores of trading ships, was full of salmon and trout and shoals of fresh-water fish. There was no shortage of work. There were brickfields, potteries, and glassworks, joiners' shops and mills, masons' yards and furniture factories, as well as row upon row of warehouses and worksheds along the river front. Latin was the universal language, written as well as spoken. The civilized citizens of Londinium were a far cry from the savage Germanic pirates and raiders from across the sea–barbarians who worshiped gods of war, who feared and hated towns as unfamiliar places where evil spirits dwelt, whose idea of luxury was an encampment under the stars and a bellyful of meat and spruce beer.

The Britons, Romanized and peaceable, were no match for such men. Although they still were held together by strong tribal loyalties and tribal customs, particularly so in the more remote areas of the island, they no longer were possessed of that warlike spirit that had fired the hearts of the Iceni tribe when they followed their Queen Boudicca into battle against the Roman conquerors long ago in the reign of the Emperor Nero. Accustomed for centuries to relying on the empire's legions to protect them, the Britons now were incapable of protecting themselves, and as the fourth century drew to its close, they grew ever more in need of protection.

The Saxons, an increasing menace, now had established settled bases along the Continental coast from which Britain could be raided more easily. In the west, the Scotti from Ireland were becoming ever more threatening under their powerful High King Niall of the Nine Hostages. Repeated raids were made along the coasts that faced the turbulent Irish Sea, and prisoners were carried off in hundreds to become the slaves of Irish chieftains. King Niall's pirates thrust as far inland as Chester, Caerleon-on-Usk, and Wroxeter, and although in 405 King Niall himself was killed at sea, the raids did not stop.

Yet even after the legions had gone and the Vandals had begun to swarm across Roman Africa under King Gaiseric, Roman Britain had not lost all hope of survival. In 429 there arrived in the island a bishop from Auxerre in Gaul, a bishop named Germanus, who had been a soldier in his youth and never had lost his taste for battle. Bishop Germanus found Britain a "most wealthy island," with still-thriving communities governed by local kings whose families had been used to kingship from ancient times. Even before the Romans occupied Britain permanently in A.D. 43, Cunobelinus, the original of Shakespeare's Cymbeline, the powerful ruler of the Catuvellauni tribe in southern Britain, used to style himself *rex*, or king, on the coins issued from his mint. With the breakdown of Roman rule, the Britons were tending more and more to honor the ancient ties and rally around their regional leaders.

Despite the constant inroads by the barbarians, Germanus found that town life still was going on. Trade in the port of Londinium remained active; in Verulamium, farther north, the Roman theater had become a refuse dump for the decaying vegetables of the market, but the shops still were open and local crafts still flourished. Germanus also found that while the invaders might destroy isolated farms near the coast, burn down the wattle-and-daub huts of peasants and the timber hovels of fishermen, trample down crops and orchards, vineyards and gardens, they were not yet capable of fighting a pitched battle or of storming the masonry walls of a Roman town or fort.

Before his arrival in Britain, Germanus had been military governor of the Armorican district of Gaul, with responsibility for guarding the Channel coast. Yet it was not as a soldier that he had been sent to Britain, but as a preacher who

could combat a new heresy called Pelagianism.
A Briton named Pelagius had begun to teach
that the soul is born in a neutral condition and
that the human will was perfectly free to make
its own choice between virtue and vice. This
idea denied the whole concept of original sin,
and the pious bishops of Rome feared that such
a teaching might undermine the authority of
the Church. Germanus, however, was as concerned with the bodies of the British people as
with their souls.

He reorganized the bands of local militia,
persuaded their leaders to appoint him their
supreme commander, or *dux*, and taught them
how to fight a formal battle. When next the
barbarians appeared, the Britons were better
prepared to meet them. Instead of retreating
inland in panic, driven like sheep before the
advancing Saxons, terrified by the shouts of
the savage throng and the braying of their war
horns, they withdrew in good order, drawing
their oppressors into the trap that Germanus
had laid for them. The Saxons marched on,
unsuspecting, into a narrow valley, and when
they had gone too far to retreat out of the
bottleneck, Germanus broke his wary silence.
Rising to his feet, he cried out at the top of
his voice, "Alleluia!" The waiting Britons took
up the cry, and to repeated shouts of "Alleluia!

Alleluia!" they rushed down both sides of the valley onto their trapped enemies. The Saxons, surprised and alarmed by this unexpected reply to their own war cries, turned on their heels and fled, dropping their spears as they ran.

It was a great victory, but only a temporary respite. The years passed, and the Saxons and their allies grew more resolute and more enterprising. They came now not only in galleys, but also in ships with leather sails, leaving their vessels concealed in coastal inlets, advancing down the neglected roads, driving ever deeper into the British countryside. They became expert at besieging and storming fortified encampments, at recognizing the weak link in a chain of defenses and battering their way through it. Soon they began to settle down on the land they formerly had been content to pillage and lay waste, and they established small farming settlements of rough huts around the wooden halls of their thanes, or lords.

In 446, the Britons made a final, forlorn plea for help from Rome. Those parts of Romanized Britain that still were able to act collectively joined in dispatching an urgent message to Aetius, the Roman general in Gaul:

To Aetius, three times consul, the groans of the Britons; the barbarians drive us to the sea, the sea drives us to the

> barbarians; between these two forms of death, we are either
> massacred or drowned.

But there was no response; Aetius had enough to do fending off barbarian inroads in Gaul itself. No help came.

Then—or so it seems from the confused and incomplete records of these times—a call was made to a leader closer to home, to Vortigern, a powerful British ruler who had gained control of an extensive district in the west of Britain and who exercised a considerable influence over the south of the island as well. According to some sources, Vortigern is supposed to have married Sevira, daughter of the Roman Emperor Maximus, and thus, though a rough and ready British-speaking overlord himself, he had some respect for Roman ways. His advice to the Britons was to bring a Roman solution to bear upon Britain's problems.

The Roman Empire had relied for the maintenance of its power not only upon recruits taken into its army from all the world's races, but also upon whole tribes, enlisted to defend particular areas. These tribes were known as *foederati*, because they had entered into a *foedus*, or treaty, with Rome; its terms usually were that they would be admitted into the empire in return for defending whatever portion of it they were allotted, and although the soldiers thus gained land within the empire, they maintained their own laws and customs and their own identities. This policy, Vortigern apparently suggested–and the British councilors agreed– should be adopted now. In return for their help in keeping at bay the Picts and Scotti and any other raiders, and on the understanding that they live at peace with their British neighbors, a war band of Saxon troops and their women were accepted and settled in the southeastern region of Britain.

According to the Venerable Bede, the Northumbrian monk and historian whose *History of the English Church and People*, completed in 731, is our chief source of knowledge for this period, the leaders of the federated troops were two Jutish chiefs, named Hengist and Horsa. They established themselves on the Isle of Thanet, an area of rich farmland separated from Kent (the land of the Cantii tribe) by a narrow channel, which was guarded at each end by a Roman fort. This was a long way distant from the areas of Britain under attack by the Picts and the Irish warbands, but it was convenient for Vortigern to keep them under his control when they were not fighting in the north, and the Saxon federates were well placed to under take coastal patrols for the protection of Londinium.

At first all went well. The Picts and Scotti were subdued; the Kentish settlement prospered; and Britain enjoyed a period of unaccustomed peace. But gradually the settlers called over friends and reinforcements–Angles, Jutes, and Saxons–from across the North Sea and began spreading themselves ever deeper into southeastern Britain. They demanded more and more land and more generous payments. At some time in the 450's, the increasingly angry quarrels between them and their British employers flared into open war. In 457, there was a ferocious battle at Crayford in Kent, and the Britons, having lost four thousand men on the field, "fled to London in great terror."

This is the last recorded mention of London for a century and a half; Britain's capital and other Roman towns in turn fell victim to the invaders, now armed with the Roman siege equipment that had fallen into their hands. The Saxons advanced farther and farther inland, devastating countryside and towns alike:

Public and private buildings were razed [according to Bede], priests were slain at the altar; bishops and people alike, regardless of rank, were destroyed with fire and sword, and none remained to bury those who had suffered a cruel death. A few wretched survivors captured in the hills were butchered wholesale, and others, desperate with hunger, came out and surrendered to the enemy for food, although they were doomed to lifelong slavery even if they escaped instant massacre. Some fled overseas in their misery; others, clinging to their homeland, eked out a wretched and fearful existence.

Bede's picture is a fearful one, yet the vast majority of survivors probably stayed close to what once had been their homes, in great discomfort and misery. Some may have sailed across the Channel to the old Roman province of Armorica, the first stage of three centuries of migration that eventually took a British (Celtic) language—and gave the modern name of Brittany—to this great Atlantic peninsula.

It was fortunate, then, that in the West Country there was a tribal leader strong enough to make a stand against the Saxon menace and to offer shelter to those who had escaped its shadow or were prepared to take up arms in defense of the old culture. This man's name was Ambrosius, a ruler who seems to have advised Vortigern of the dangers of the Saxon and to have managed to stand aloof from its consequences.

Ambrosius apparently was of Roman descent. The land over which he ruled was certainly as Romanized as any in Britain and probably remained so, even at this time, preserving what it could of the traditions of Roman culture and organizing both its government and its army on the Roman model. Although the Saxon warrior Aelle landed near Selsey in 477 and carved out for himself the kingdom of the South Saxons (which has given its name to the present-day county of Sussex), and although in 495 Cerdic landed on the shore of Southampton Water to found the kingdom of the West Saxons (which later would become King Alfred's kingdom of Wessex), farther to the west the Romano-British kingdom of Ambrosius remained secure. To this haven, says the earliest of British historians, a monk named Gildas, writing in the sixth-century, men from the other threatened tribes of Britain flocked "as eagerly as bees when a storm is brewing."

For the time being, Ambrosius prevented the storm from breaking over his kingdom. A contemporary writer on the Continent described Britain in the 480's as being prosperous and peaceful despite the Saxon incursions. By 500, there was a considerable settlement of Saxons along the east coast (Essex), and the kingdoms of Sussex and Wessex continued to flourish and expand. Yet in the Cotswold Hills, along the borders of Wales, and in Dumnonia (the peninsula occupied today by the counties of Devon and Cornwall) Roman Britain contrived to live on.

Both written records and archaeological
evidence for even the most superficial history
of Britain at this time are tantalizingly sparse.
Nevertheless, it is possible to build a credible
picture, from what few materials do exist, of
what life probably was like in the western area
of Britain loyal to Ambrosius.

Some sort of seaborne trade was maintained
with such Atlantic ports as Bordeaux and Nantes
and with the Mediterranean—increasingly so
after about 500. Small amounts of wine, in pottery amphoras (jars), and perhaps cooking oil as
well, came in the ships of the traders. Early writ-
ings suggest that corn, woolen goods, and hides,
perhaps Irish wolfhounds (which evidently were
highly prized for their speed and strength), and
perhaps even slaves, were exported in return.

In a few centers like Gloucester, life may
have been carried on in the old Roman way,
with Latin still the language of a household
proud of its links with the past, treasuring its
manuscripts, its silver and pewter tableware, its
civilized methods of worship—whether the belief
was in Christ or in some pagan gods.

But in most of Ambrosius' kingdom people
had reverted to a less Romanized way of life,
grouped together in small communities like the
hill forts of their ancestors, using native pottery
that was made by hand—not thrown on the wheel

like the Roman ware—and speaking, a variety of British dialects. For the poor, as always, life was hard. Living in huts of stone and thatch, laboriously tilling their small square fields, attempting to improve their plain diet of bread and occasional pieces of meat with strong herbs, dressed in rough woolen clothes, such people would, have had little cause to celebrate the pleasures of human existence. Yet they valued their freedom and their sense of national identity—and they were prepared to fight for them.

Perhaps to protect themselves against Saxon invasion, possibly to protect their cattle from raids, either by the Saxons or by other British tribes, the inhabitants of this last enclave of Romano-British civilization threw up a series of linear earthworks. One of the largest of these is known today as the Wansdyke, a huge manmade ridge, that stretches fifty miles from Inkpen in what is now Berkshire, across Savernake Forest and the Marlborough Downs, over a Roman road that used to lead into Bath, and on down toward the Bristol Channel. Historians are uncertain of its purpose, but its presence, rising up from the peaceful fields of the modern English countryside, is a reminder of some tremendous joint effort by people who can have had only the most primitive implements to aid them.

Under Ambrosius the Britons suffered set-backs and defeats, but they won victories, too. They may have lost ground occasionally, but they never were driven into serious retreat. They had a cause and they had a leader. Yet men were bound to wonder what would happen when that leader died, as he was bound to. Could anyone replace Ambrosius? Could any man be a more memorable leader?

4

"Commander in the Battles"

In those days [that followed the death of Ambrosius], the Saxons grew in numbers and prospered in Britain... Then Arthur the warrior and the kings of the Britons fought against the Saxons, but Arthur himself was the *dux bellorum*, the commander in the battles. The first battle was on the mouth of the river which is called Glein. The second, the third, the fourth, and the fifth upon another river, which is called Dubglass, and is in the region of Linnuis. The sixth battle was upon the river which is called Bassas.

The seventh battle was in the wood of Celidon, that is Cat Coit Celidon. The eighth was the battle by the castle of Guinnion, in which Arthur carried upon his shoulders an image of the Blessed Mary, the Eternal Virgin. And the heathen were turned to flight on that day, and great was the slaughter brought upon them through the virtue of our Lord, Jesus Christ, and through the virtue of the Blessed Virgin, His Mother.

The ninth battle was fought in the City of the Legion. The tenth battle was waged on the banks of the river which is called Tribruit. The eleventh battle was fought in the mountain which is called Agned. The twelfth battle was on Mount Badon where in one day nine hundred and sixty men fell in one onslaught of Arthur's. And no one laid them low but himself alone. And in all these battles he stood out as victor.

Thus Arthur makes his first appearance in a historical chronicle. Its compiler was the Welsh monk Nennius, who was writing in the ninth century; the work is the same *Historia Brittonum* that relates the "marvels" of the stone that bears the footprint of Arthur's dog Cabal and of the mysterious mound that marks the grave of Arthur's son Anir.

But although these marvels may defy belief, Nennius is more credible when he comes to this list of twelve victories won by Arthur as commander of the British forces. For while some of the places named by Nennius no longer are identifiable, some guesses have been made as to the location of the others, based on the ninth century Welsh form of the place names. It is impossible now to identify the sites of Castle Guinnion, the mountain called Agned, or the River Bassas, but it has been assumed that the region of Linnuis could be the Lindsey area of Lincolnshire south of the Humber and that the River Glein is the Lincolnshire River Glen. This certainly would support the belief that Arthur may have been called upon to campaign against the Saxons and Angles who were landing in increasing numbers on the east coast of Britain in the early sixth century–giving their name to the area now known as East Anglia. The wood of Celidon probably is the forest of Caledonia in the wild Scottish uplands beyond Hadrian's Wall, where a campaign against the Picts was fought at about this time. The City of the Legion probably is Chester. Mount Badon has been variously identified with Badbury near Swindon in Wiltshire, Badbury Hill in Berkshire, Badbuiy Rings near Blandford in Dorset, and Bedwyn near Inkpen–but in any case, it is believed to be somewhere in southern Britain in the neighborhood of the Wansdyke. Wherever it was, Mount Badon obviously must have been the site of a battle or siege of supreme importance. We may picture Arthur's troops surrounding the steep and strongly fortified hill, cutting off the supplies from the enemy who occupied it, forcing them to break out, and then slaughtering them as they tried to escape.

Because the list of battles appears to range so widely across the country, some historians have held it to be suspect, believing that it is more likely that the battles took place in one area, the north, for instance, or the southwest. But if they ranged all over Britain, this would bear out the belief that Arthur was indeed the supreme military leader that Nennius' description of a *dux bellorum* implies–that he took his army from river to river and from coast to coast to fight the invaders whenever and wherever they seemed most threatening.

The suggestion has been made that Arthur's defense of Britain may have been conducted on the basis of a system developed by the Romans in the previous century, when the island was divided into four smaller provinces and its military organization into three commands. The Dux Britanniarum (the duke of the Britains), who had his headquarters at York, was responsible for defending the northern frontier against the Picts and Scotti; the Comes Litoris Saxonici (the count of the Saxon Shore) defended the southeasterncoast from the Germanic pirates aided by a well-built and strongly garrisoned series of forts that stretched from the Wash to the Isle of Wight. Both these leaders commanded a local militia of garrison troops, and their duties essentially were to hold the frontier line. The third leader, the Comes Britanniarum (the count of the Britains) was entrusted with the direction of a field army of six cavalry and three infantry units, an army that was mobile, able to come to the defense of his colleagues when the need arose.

It is significant that the army under the count's command was composed chiefly of cavalry. The Roman army, in its early days, had made little use of cavalry, preferring to rely on the superb discipline and fighting strength of its infantry, grouped in legions some six thousand strong. Gradually, however, as the Roman generals came in contact with barbarian troops using cavalry armed with bows and spears, they had begun to incorporate cavalry into their own commands. Usually these were lightly armed auxiliary units, made up of *foederati* fighting under the eagles, but also there were mailed cavalry, known as *cataphracti* or *clibanarii*. The *cataphracts*, whose name comes from a Greek word meaning "covered in mail," wore helmets and body armor made of iron scales or chain mail, with arm- and leg-pieces attached to it. The *clibanarii*, so called from the Latin word for "baking pan," were armed from head to foot in scales or mail, and their horses, too, wore protective trappings of iron scales sewn on blankets—a heavy and cumbersome uniform, especially in hot weather. Both types of cavalry were armed with long, heavy spears and swords, and they could slash their way through poorly organized enemy troops with terrible effect.

As the responsibility of defending Rome's frontiers came to demand a more flexible type of army, the Roman legions had been reorganized into smaller units, of about one thousand men to a legion, while the cavalry became a separate arm of the service. Essentially, the need was for mobility, so that the troops could be thrown into action speedily where they were needed most.

The situation in Britain also was one that demanded mobility, and it has been suggested plausibly that Arthur served in some capacity resembling that of a count of the Britains, deploying a small force of cavalry, which may or may not have been armored, but which, like its Roman predecessors, was professionally disciplined and extremely effective in dealing with Saxon foes who had no horses and who fought with great bravery, but little organization.

As commander in chief, then, ranging far and wide with his band of "knights," Arthur would have been directing a campaign on whose success the whole of Britain's freedom and future depended. He would have been the one man capable of organizing the island's defense against the heathen invaders, the one leader capable of inspiring his people to fight to the death. But if this were the reason for Nennius' calling him *dux bellorum*, what about the incidental details in the historian's account? Neither the mention of his going into battle with an image of the Virgin Mary on his shoulder, nor the feat of killing nine hundred sixty men singlehandedly is easy to accept literally. But it could be that when Nennius wrote, he had before him an old text that he misread. To this day, the Welsh word for "shoulder," *ysgwydd*, is almost identical with the word meaning "shield," *ysgwyd*, and it is not difficult to suppose that the Celtic words should have been similar also, if not identical. It certainly seems more probable that Arthur would have gone into battle bearing a shield on which was some badge proclaiming his faith in the Blessed Mother.

As for the remarkably large number of victims slain by Arthur at Mount Badon, the distinction might be simply that Arthur and his men were fighting this battle, not in conjunction with other British leaders, but alone against the Saxons and that Nennius probably was describing an overwhelming defeat inflicted by Arthur's cavalry alone.

It also is possible, as another writer has suggested, that Nennius was following an early

Welsh poem that listed Arthur's battles and that the curiously precise number *nine hundred sixty* would become, in Welsh, "three hundreds and three twenties," an appropriate figure for a hero whose strength already was legendary in a poetry whose early forms were obsessed with the number *three*.

The next references to a historical Arthur occur in the Latin lists of events and the years in which they took place called the *Annales Cambriae*. These probably were compiled in the north of Britain about the middle of the tenth century, but they are derived from sources at least as early as those used by Nennius. These "annals of Wales," which cover the years 453 to 954, mention only the last of Arthur's battles as named by Nennius, under the date 516: "The battle of Badon in which Arthur carried the cross of Our Lord Jesus Christ, for three days and three nights on his shoulders, and the Britons were victorious." (Here again, the reference to Arthur carrying the cross on his shoulders may reflect a Welsh confusion between shoulders and shields.) Under the date 537 there is a second reference to Arthur, this time to the battle fought between him and his illegitimate son Mordred that forms the climax of the *Morte d'Arthur*: "The battle of Camlann in which Arthur and Medraut were slain; and there was death in England."

Nowhere yet is there any suggestion that Arthur was a king. But his name, which in its Latin form is Artorius, suggests that he may have been of distinguished birth and from a family in some way connected with Rome. More than one Roman named Artorius lived in Britain during the empire's heyday, and one, Lucius Artorius Castus, led the sixth legion on an expedition to Armorica in the middle of the second century. It has been conjectured that an ancestor of the British Arthur may have served under him and that, proud of this service, he gave his son his leader's name, which thereafter was handed down in his family from generation to generation. But such a conjecture is not really necessary. The name Artorius implies that Arthur was of Roman descent, and the fact that he succeeded Ambrosius as leader implies that Arthur may well have been a relation of Ambrosius. According to Geoffrey of Monmouth, Ambrosius was Uther Pendragon's brother and therefore Arthur's uncle—although Uther is probably a figment of Geoffrey's lively imagination and no earlier chronicle supports this claim to royal birth. Another possibility is that after his triumph over the Saxons Arthur's men might have named their leader king, following the example of Roman legions in fourth-century Britain who proclaimed their general, Maximus, emperor.

It is not until the late eleventh century that Arthur appears regularly and unequivocally as a king. He does so in several lives of Celtic priests and monks upon whom the Welsh and Britons somewhat freely bestowed the title of saint. In more than one of the lives, however, Arthur is called a tyrant king, and presented as a ruffianly ruler with little respect for the church, or as a *rex rebellus*, who remains evil until converted by some miracle worked by the saint whose holy career is presented for the reader's admiration and improvement. Although few of these tales about King Arthur are remotely credible, they do at least show that the monks who wrote them realized that any connection with him, however strange or fanciful, would lend credit and renown to their own, now forgotten, saintly heroes. Their less than attractive presentation of Arthur also may provide a clue to a mysterious omission in the earliest surviving chronicle of the period in which we believe him to have lived—the inference being that Arthur had in some way offended the Church in his fight for Britain's freedom.

This chronicle, *De Excidio et Conquestu Britanniae*, is the work of a sixth-century monk named Gildas. He probably was writing only a few years after Arthur's death—he may even have known Arthur. Yet he never once mentions his name.

Gildas was the son of a minor British chieftain whose small domain in Scotland was overrun constantly by Pictish marauders. He and most of his several brothers abandoned their homeland and emigrated to Wales, where they sought and were given the protection of King Caedwalla of Gwynedd. Gildas married in Wales, but his wife died young and he turned to a religious life. At various times in his career he seems to have lived in Ireland, on a lonely island in the Bristol Channel–where he lived as a hermit on fish and gulls' eggs–in Brittany, and at Glastonbury in Somerset. On his death, he was deemed worthy to be considered a saint.

His main work, the *De Excidio et Conquestu Britanniae*, was written in about 540. He himself refers to it as a *liber querulus*, a book of complaints. It castigates his contemporaries for their lack of foresight and for their blindness to the lessons of the past; it attacks the local kings of Britain for immorality and tyranny. "They have many wives, and all of them adulteresses and prostitutes. They often take oaths, and always break them. They wage wars, and the wars are unjust on their own countrymen. They hunt down thieves in the countryside, but they have thieves at their own tables, whom they love and load with gifts…"

Gildas briefly summarizes the historical events that led up to this appalling state of affairs. He ends with a great victory over the Saxons in a battle that he says was fought in the year of his birth, that is, in about 500; and this victory put an end to foreign wars, though not to civil wars. The name of this decisive victory is the Siege of Mount Badon–the last of the twelve victories attributed to Arthur by Nennius, and the famous battle in which, so the *Annales Cambriae* record, Arthur carried the cross of Christ for three days and three nights. But Gildas says nothing of Arthur, to whom the chronicles give credit for the victory, referring merely and very briefly to the battle at which there was no small slaughter of those "gallows-birds," the Saxons.

This strange omission led some later historians to believe that there was no such man as Arthur. Some suggested that the whole Arthurian epic was a fabrication, a characteristic result of wishful thinking at a time when a national hero was desperately needed, or an attribution to one man of the virtues and achievements of a score of lesser men who fought against the powers of darkness. It was true, went the argument, that Gildas did not mention many names in his text; but the name of Ambrosius was given. Why not the name of Arthur, then, if it really was Arthur who had won a victory so complete that Britain had been granted peace for almost half a century?

The question has at least two answers, both of which are credible. One could be that Gildas may have had some good reason for not naming Arthur directly and that instead he mentioned him in an oblique way that his contemporaries would have understood, although we do not.

Gildas refers in his attacks on the wicked rulers of his time to one Welsh king, Cuneglasus, who was a "despiser of God, an adulterer, and an oppressor of monks." Yet in the better days of his youth Cuneglasus had driven "the chariot which carried The Bear." Who was this great man, known as The Bear, who should have a prince of royal blood to drive his chariot? Gildas does not say. But the Celtic word for "bear" is *arth* or *artos*.

There also is the possibility that Gildas did not mention Arthur by name because Arthur, like so many of his contemporaries, had fallen short of the monk's strict ideals in religion and morals and that Gildas had quarreled with him.

Arthur might also, like Cuneglasus, have been considered an "oppressor of monks." Fighting the Saxons was a costly enterprise, and a war leader who ranged as far as Arthur presumably did must have had occasion often to call upon monasteries for help in providing money and food for his men and fodder for his horses. Frequently he must have been forced to seize what was not given freely. Such high-handed impositions certainly could account for the unsympathetic figure Arthur cuts in the later saints' lives that already have been mentioned.

But there may have been something more personal in the quarrel–if quarrel indeed there was–between Gildas and Arthur. According to a biography of Gildas, written in the twelfth century in Llancarfan Abbey, where Gildas himself had once lived, Arthur had killed Hueil, Gildas' eldest brother. Hueil had not gone to Wales, like the rest of his family, but had remained in Scotland to inherit his father's lands. He had come, it seems, to some traitorous understanding with the Picts in order to secure possession of his kingdom. Thus Arthur made war on him. Hueil was defeated and slain, and Gildas, who had in the past "diligently loved Arthur," now turned against him as the cause of his beloved brother's death. A similar story also appears in another eleventh-century Welsh tale, which indicates at least that Gildas' biographer did not invent the story of the quarrel. If there is any truth in the story, if Gildas and Arthur did find themselves on opposite sides in the civil wars that followed the battle of Mount Badon and that led to the fight between Arthur and Mordred at Camlann, then Gildas' reluctance to mention his brother's destroyer is explained. He could scarcely deny the triumph of Mount Badon, but he could not bring himself to record the name of the victor. There is also a long standing tradition that Gildas did, in fact, write about Arthur but later threw the book that included his name into the sea.

In the end, though, it may not even be necessary to find farfetched reasons for the fact that Arthur's name does not appear in the *De Excidio*. If the battle of Mount Badon was as resounding a victory as all accounts suggest that it was, its details would be perfectly well, known to all the book's readers. Gildas had no need to repeat the information that Arthur had won it–it would have been a fact of life, taken for granted by everyone.

Certainly, by the time Nennius was writing, two hundred fifty years later, Arthur had been accepted as the victor at Mount Badon and as the paragon of British heroes. Not only in Britain was this so, but also in Brittany, where so many Britons had fled after the Saxon invasions. They took with them stirring stories of the mighty warrior, marvelous tales that later were embellished and adapted to the taste of the people in whose land they settled. But the basic material remained surprisingly close to the Celtic legends and poems of Wales and the British West Country, where Arthur's great deeds were treasured and his praises sung. The common people, the descendants of the Britons Arthur had fought to defend, never lost faith in the leader who had been their champion. Indeed, over the years their belief became still more fervent.

> If you do not believe me [wrote a twelfth-century French theologian], go to the realm of Armorica [to Brittany] which is lesser Britain, and preach about the market places and villages that Arthur the Briton is dead as other men are dead, and facts themselves will show you how true is Merlin's prophecy, which says that the ending of Arthur shall be doubtful. Hardly will you escape unscathed, without being overwhelmed by the curses or crushed by the stones of your hearers.

By the twelfth century, as we have seen, Arthur's fame had spread far beyond Britain and Brittany—to France, to Germany, and to Italy. The sixth-century British warrior whose true self long since had been obscured by the mists of time had become one of the most celebrated heroes of Christendom. To the peasant he was the just protector, who one day would rise again to right their wrongs; to his lord Arthur was the model of knightly virtue; to all men Arthur's courage offered hope, and his prowess inspiration. Naturally, proof of his existence was sought–yet proof, beyond the brief mentions in the chronicles, was strangely lacking. Then, in 1191, the skeptics suddenly were confounded by a remarkable discovery, which seemed to establish Arthur once and for all as an actual historical figure.

This discovery was made in the heart of the West Country–Arthur's traditional realm–at Glastonbury in Somerset, known in local lore as the Isle of Avalon, to which Arthur was borne, after the fateful battle of Camlann, for the healing of his grievous wound.

Once Glastonbury was, indeed, an island. In earlier times the waters of the Bristol Channel had reached deep into the Somerset levels, covering great stretches with shallow tidal water, amid which the present hills and ridges stood up like islands. In the midst of this expanse, at Glastonbury, the Iron Age British of the second century B.C. built themselves villages of timber huts on patches of dry land and fortified them against wild animals and other marauders. The so-called lake village at Glastonbury rested on timber platforms, supported by massive posts driven into the marsh and peat.

The people who lived here, in circular huts of wood and clay with roofs of reed thatch, were far from being a barbarous community. They were skillful farmers who grew wheat and barley, peas and beans; they were expert carpenters, wood carvers, and basket makers; they were expert, too, in metalwork and pottery, even in glasswork. Although they were under steadily increasing pressure from Belgic warrior tribes, who had crossed over from northeastern Gaul to settle in Britain, they managed to maintain this astonishingly high standard of civilization for more than a century. Then, shortly before the first Romans landed in Britain, in B.C., the village was attacked by a powerful force of Belgic raiders, all its buildings were destroyed, and most of its people were massacred.

The peace that Roman power brought to Britain enabled the survivors of the massacre to move away to drier and more healthy ground, and Glastonbury probably became once more the deserted swamp it had been before the lake village was built. Over the centuries, however, there were changes in sea level that had the effect of partially draining the marsh, and at some period in early Christian times–no one knows when, but it certainly was well before the end of the sixth century–a monastery was built there. Its monks used to claim that the Glastonbuy monastery was the oldest such foundation in Britain, and the supposed original abbey church, the Vetusta Ecclesia, a primitive construction of wattle and daub, was reverently shown to the crowds of pilgrims who flocked to Glastonbury to see "the source and fountain of all religion" in Britain.

It certainly was shown to William of Malmesbury, the most reliable of all twelfth-century historians, when he visited Glastonbury at some date between 1125 and 1135. He seems to have entertained some doubts about its age and authenticity, but he was sufficiently impressed by the abbey's ancient documents to put on record his opinion that the Church of St. Mary at Glastonbury was indeed "the first church in the kingdom of Britain."

Delighted to have confirmation of their most ancient foundation from so respected an authority as William of Malmesbury, the monks at Glastonbury made and circulated several copies of his *De Antiquitate Glastoniensis Ecclesiae*. Indeed, they went further than this: they issued new and altered editions of the work, leaving William's name on the title page but adding new material to the abbey's greater credit. Included was an account of how the abbey definitely had been founded by "no other hands than those of the disciples of Christ," who had come to England in 63 A.D. to preach the Gospel. The group was led by Joseph of Arimathea, the follower of Jesus who had begged Christ's body from Pilate and laid it to rest in the sepulcher. A British king, impressed by their conduct, gave them land on which to settle at Glastonbury. There they were visited by the Archangel Gabriel, who told them to build a church of boughs, the original of the Vetusta Ecclesia, to be dedicated to the Virgin Mary.

Gradually, as new editions of William's book were issued by succeeding generations of monks, each copy written and illuminated with infinite care and artistry, further details were added. St. Joseph of Arimathea had brought with him to Glastonbury, if not the Holy Grail itself, at least a pair of stoppered vessels, one containing the blood, the other the sweat of Christ, and these two vessels had been buried with him in the abbey grounds. At the foot of Glastonbury Tor, the hill that rises so steeply above the abbey, St. Joseph had knelt to pray, leaning on his staff as he did so, and the staff immediately had taken root and budded. This was the origin of the celebrated Glastonbury Thorn, which flowered every year at Christmas and continued to do so until a Puritan cut it down and burned it in the seventeenth century. (It did not die out altogether, however, for cuttings taken from it have continued to the present day to bloom within a week of Christmas.) Most important of all for our story, although William of Malmesbury himself never had linked the name of Arthur

THE QUEST OF THE HOLY GRAIL
BY EDWIN AUSTIN ABBEY

Edwin Austin Abbey was one of the most extraordinary American artists of the late nineteenth and early twentieth centuries. He was born in Philadelphia in 1852 and studied at the Pennsylvania Academy of the Fine Arts. He achieved fame for his magazine illustrations, which were noteworthy for their rich detail and classical themes. In 1878, he moved to England where, in 1898, he was elected to the Royal Academy. When he died in 1911, he was regarded as one of the greatest artists of his time. In 1889, Abbey became involved in mural illustration, and in 1890, he was commissioned to decorate fifteen panels in the delivery room of the Boston Public Library. He chose as his subject one of the great legends in the Arthurian romances, Sir Galahad's epic journey to find the Holy Grail. *The Quest of the Holy Grail* was installed in 1895 in what is now known as the Abbey Room. In fifteen richly detailed murals, Abbey presents important events in the quest, from Galahad's birth, to his knighthood, his trials and adventures, and his ultimate success. What follows is a rare publication of the entire fifteen-panel story.

In *The Vision* (above), an angel, left, presents the Holy Grail to the baby Galahad, right center, so that he can drink from it. Galahad is held by his mother, who has turned her face away so that she does not see the angel.

The second illustration in the mural is *The Oath of Knighthood*. In it Galahad, far right, kneels as he takes his oath of knighthood. Behind him, the knights Sir Lancelot and Sir Bors fasten onto his feet the spurs of knighthood. Looking on are nuns holding tapers. Galahad wears red, the color of purity, throughout the murals.

The third illustration is *The Round Table*. It shows Sir Galahad, left, being led to the Seat Perilous, far right, by a white robed man, middle. Standing beside the Seat Perilous and beckoning toward it is King Arthur. In the background, the Knights of the Order of the Round Table sit around the Round Table. Standing above and behind everyone is a host of angels, watching. According to legend, only someone pure of soul could safely sit on the Seat Perilous. When Galahad did so, the chair became known as the "Seat of Galahad."

In *The Departure*, the kneeling Knights of the Round Table receive a benediction from a priest, standing at left, prior to their departure to begin the quest to find the Holy Grail. Galahad is in the front of the group.

In *Castle of the Grail*, Amfortas the heavily cloaked Fisher King, center, lies on a gilded bed. In the background, left, stands Galahad. The Damsel with the Golden Dish, and bearer of the Grail, right, is entering the chamber, in which are already gathered men and women who searched for the Grail but, because they had not attained perfection, couldn't see it, even when it was in their midst. Galahad, too, is unable to see the Grail, because he has not yet given up all worldly desires.

In *The Loathly Damsel* a kneeling and praying Galahad is accosted by three approaching women, led by the Loathly Damsel, herself, in a hooded cloak and riding a mule. She cradles in her arm the severed head of a king. According to legend, the Loathly Damsel was once a beautiful woman. A curse laid on her rendered her bald and hideous. As a result, she hides her face beneath a hood. Against her will, she is cursed to use her magic power to tempt and destroy any knight or king she encounters. Galahad successfully escapes from her.

In *Conquest of the Seven Deadly Sins*, Galahad, left, attacks the seven Knights of Darkness. At his feet lies the body of one slain evil knight. The seven represent the seven deadly sins: pride, envy, gluttony, lust, anger, greed, and sloth. The evil knights have captured and imprisoned a large group of maidens, the Virtues. Galahad fights the knights to defeat sin, free the maidens, and restore virtue to the world.

Key to the Castle shows a kneeling Galahad with his sword drawn, left, accepting the key to the castle from a white-robed monk. Having stain all the evil knights, Galahad is now ready to free the imprisoned maidens.

In *Castle of the Maidens Galahad*, left of center, takes the outstretched hands of some of the maidens, the Virtues, who have gathered to greet their liberator. Galahad's arrival has been expected, for it was prophesied that only a perfect knight would rescue them. Having freed the maidens, Galahad returns to his quest for the Grail.

In *Galahad Parts from His Bride, Blanchefleur*, Galahad, right, walks down steps away from his bride, the seated Blanchefleur, at left. A squire waits at the open door, holding Galahad's shield. Blanchefleur is still in her wedding dress, an indication that this is their wedding day. Because only a virgin knight can find the Holy Grail, Galahad must leave his bride before their marriage is consummated. This sacrifice of his last worldly desire, earthly love as represented by Blanchfleur, is the final act that will permit him to achieve his goal of finding the Grail.

In *Death of Amfortas* Galahad, center, holds a dying Amfortas. Behind them both hovers an angel, who is carrying away the Holy Grail to the place where Galahad will be permitted to find it. Galahad's success in renouncing all worldly desires has freed the curse that has kept Amfortas alive.

In *Galahad the Deliverer* we see Galahad, on a white horse, carrying his standard through a lush countryside. People from the area are cheering and praying for him. Galahad's trip through their land has helped transform the blighted region to one of peace and prosperity.

In *Voyage to Sarras* Galahad kneels and prays, flanked by the knights Sir Bors and Sir Percival. They are sailing in Solomon's Ship, which is guided by the angel carrying the Holy Grail at far right. Sir Bors and Sir Percival have not achieved Galahad's level of purity in their souls, so they cannot find and behold the Grail, but because of their devotion to the quest they have been allowed to make the last stage of the journey with him.

The long narrow painting *The City of Sarras* shows the port of the mythical city of Sarras, with ships docked in its harbor. Dominating the scene is Galahad's shield emblazoned with the Christian cross, and behind the shield, Galahad's sword. It is here in Sarras that Galahad will finally see the Holy Grail.

In *Golden Tree and the Achievement of the Grail* a kneeling Galahad stares up at the Grail as it is raised heavenward by a white-robed Joseph of Arimathea, center. Behind them stand a half-circle of angels. Between Galahad and Joseph a golden vessel bears a cluster of golden branches. Galahad created a sacred place where he constructed this Golden Tree, and upon its completion, the Holy Grail was finally revealed to him.

with Glastonbury, it eventually appeared from later versions of his book that the king, a benefactor and patron of the abbey, actually was buried there, in the grounds that once had been known as the Isle of Avalon.

William certainly had mentioned Arthur in another work, his great history of England, *De Gestis Regum Anglorum*, in which he wrote of him as a man "truly worthy to be celebrated…since for a long time he sustained the declining fortunes of his country, and incited the unbroken spirit of the people to war. Finally, at the battle of Mount Badon, relying upon the image of the Mother of the Lord which he had fixed upon his armour, he made heed single handed against nine hundred of the enemy and routed them with incredible slaughter." But William had taken pains to separate the real Arthur from the fanciful figure of Celtic legend and romance—those "foolish dreams of deceitful fables," as he called them—and he went on to state that "the grave of Arthur is nowhere known."

The Glastonbury monks, however, cast such caution aside. Geoffrey of Monmouth's *History of the Kings of Britain* had been completed in 1139, within a few years of William of Malmesbury's visit to Glastonbury, and had made the name of King Arthur revered throughout most of the Christian world. Who could blame them for giving authority to the local tradition that Arthur had been laid to rest at Glastonbury? And what Englishman could not feel gratified when, in 1191, it appeared that their faith had been rewarded at last by proof?

The story of the monks' discovery began on May 25, 1184, when a fierce fire broke out in the abbey, destroying nearly all its buildings and its precious relics, including the old church. The tragedy was complete; but the monks were resourceful men. Encouraged by King Henry III, who agreed to contribute a substantial sum for the rebuilding of the abbey, they set about the task of raising money themselves. They went out into the country to beg; they solicited subscriptions from wealthy nobles; they recovered as many as they could of the relics that had been burned and exhibited them in shrines where pilgrims could bring their offerings. They managed to find the remains of several saints, including the bones of St. Patrick, the apostle of Ireland, and a skeleton that they claimed to be that of St. Dunstan, a former abbot of Glastonbury and Archbishop of Canterbury—a claim that aroused much indignation at Canterbury, where the monks had been showing St. Dunstan's tomb to pilgrims for over two hundred years.

The Glastonbury monks collected enough money to begin making plans for rebuilding on a most lavish scale; and by 1186, the first stage of the work was completed with the dedication of a new Lady Chapel. But in 1189 Henry II died, and his successor, Richard I, had no money to spare to rebuild abbeys in England while there were Saracens to fight in the Holy Land. Apparently the idea already had been formed of a search for King Arthur's tomb. The monks now went to work in earnest—and it was nothing less than Arthur's grave that in 1191 they claimed to have discovered.

The story of the discovery is related by Giraldus Cambrensis (Gerald of Wales), a contemporary historian who visited the abbey soon afterward and met the abbot. Giraldus may be considered a reliable authority, for he refused to accept the truth of much of the Arthurian legend and condemned Geoffrey of Monmouth for propagating the fancies that had appeared in the *History of the Kings of Britain*.

According to Giraldus, the monks at Glastonbury were given an indication of where to search by Henry II himself, who had been told by "an ancient Welsh bard, a singer of the past, that they would find the body at least sixteen feet beneath the earth, not in a tomb of stone, but in a hollow oak." It had been buried at such a depth "that it might not by any means be discovered by the Saxons, who occupied the island after his death, whom he had so often in his life defeated and almost utterly destroyed."

The monks roped off an area in the abbey grounds, erected a screen around it, and began to dig. They had gone but a foot or two when a spade struck against a slab of stone. Beneath the stone was a lead cross, and on the side of the cross that faced the stone were letters roughly incised.

The letters spelled out this legend in Latin:

HIC IACET SEPUILTUS INCLYTUS REX
ARTHURUS CUM WENNEVERIA UXORE SUA
SECUNDA IN INSULA AVALLONIA

*Here lies buried the renowned King Arthur with Guinevere his
second wife in the Isle of Avalon*

Excavating farther in growing excitement, the monks hit upon a length of hard wood. They pushed the soil away to reveal a vast coffin fashioned from a hollow oak trunk; and bursting open the lid with an iron bar, they found inside a collection of bones, the bones of an enormously tall and strong man at one end of the coffin and those of a woman at the other. The skull of the woman still was encircled by "a yellow tress of hair still retaining its colour and its freshness"; but when a monk eagerly reached down to touch the hairs, they crumbled into dust at the touch of his fingers and he himself lost his balance and fell into the grave, covering himself with mud and clay.

The bones of the man were recovered less clumsily; and as each one appeared, the monks marveled at the size of them. His shin bone, Giraldus concludes his account, "when placed against that of the tallest man in the place, and planted in the earth near his foot, reached, as the Abbot showed us, a good three inches above his knee. And the skull was so large and capacious as to be a portent or a prodigy, for the eye-socket was a good palm in width. Moreover, there were ten wounds or more, all of which were scarred over, save one larger than the rest, which had made a great hole."

Arthur and Guinevere had been found at last! Now Glastonbury Abbey could be sure of throng upon throng of visitors and pilgrims bearing gifts throughout the ensuing years. Slowly the new buildings rose toward the sky, replacing those destroyed in the recent fire; a church that eventually would be the largest in England took its splendid shape—the sprawling ruins of this beautiful abbey may be seen still. And in 1278, on the occasion of a visit to Glastonbury by King Edward I and Queen Eleanor, the remains of Arthur and Guinevere moved reverently to a black marble tomb in the center of the choir and there laid to rest. Two stone lions were placed at each end of the tomb, a statue of King Arthur at the foot, and the leaden cross found in the original tomb was placed above it, to indicate to the pilgrims of succeeding centuries where Britain's hero lay.

The tomb remained undisturbed until the sixteenth century, when Henry VIII proclaimed the dissolution of all Britain's monasteries. The abbey's lands passed into private hands, and the buildings were allowed to fall into ruins. In time both the shrine and the original site of Arthur's grave were lost; and in the eighteenth century the lead cross, too, disappeared. The story of the monks' remarkable discovery came to be derided as a typical medieval fraud.

Certainly, the lead cross was not a sixth-century one. A drawing made of it by a seventeenth-century historian who had seen it shows a script of a much later date. In addition, the reference to Arthur as king indicates that it was made long after his death at a time when his kingship had become part of the legend. It is impossible to be certain about the bones; they may have been those of a gigantic Iron Age warrior and his woman, buried in a dugout canoe from the Glastonbury lake village after its destruction by the Belgae. The monks may have found them by chance while digging a grave; or they could have found them elsewhere and placed them in the spot most convenient for their discovery.

In addition, the Abbot of Glastonbury and his monks were not alone in wanting to make the discovery of Arthur's tomb; King Henry II also was interested, although he himself died before it actually was found. Potential trouble was stirring in Wales, whose people were in a constant state of rebellion. The legends of Arthur's survival were known to all Welshmen: there was real danger that a rebel leader might arouse widespread support by declaring that he was Arthur risen again to lead them against their Norman oppressors. It would be a wise precaution to offer proof to these descendants of the Britons that Arthur really was dead.

Yet in recent years, the monks' story has been shown not to be a complete fabrication. In 1934, an archaeological team digging in the abbey ruins came across the base of King Arthur's shrine; and in 1962, another team identified the site of a grave that must be the one the monks claimed to have dug up. It is possible that it was indeed Arthur's grave, and that it originally had been marked as such by the stone slab that the monks discovered, but that over the years the stone had been covered by earth and the site lost to view. The cross could have been placed beneath the stone when the grave was marked as Arthur's, say, in the tenth century, when St. Dunstan was Abbot. Experts contend that its lettering could have been done then, and certainly the placing of lead crosses in graves was a common tenth-century practice.

There is also the fact that the other Glastonbury claims were quickly discredited, as Geoffrey Ashe, a well-known writer on the Arthurian legend, has pointed out:

The bones of St. Patrick and St. Dunstan were denounced as spurious by indignant voices from Ireland and Canterbury. But the Welsh made no comment on the depressing exhumation of their national chief. They offered no alternative legend, they produced no counter-Avalon [indeed, no place in Britain other than Glastonbury ever has claimed to be the Isle of Avalon], such an acquiescent hush has its own eloquence. It hints at a long-standing tradition of Arthur's death and interment in the monastery, not widely familiar, but so fully accepted...that once the secret was out the English assertions could not be denied.

In any case, the 1962 discovery of the site of the grave, whether Arthur's or not, was the first of a series of archaeological finds that now are combining to suggest that much more of the Arthurian legend may rest on fact than ever before has been supposed.

5

The Quest for Camelot

The discovery in 1962 of the apparent site of Arthur's grave at Glastonbury led to renewed interest in the whole of that area of Somerset, particularly, in the persistent legend that the hill known as South Cadbury Castle, twelve miles southeast of Glastonbury, was once the famous Camelot, site of King Arthur's court.

In the early sixteenth century, the antiquarian John Leland visited the sleepy little village of South Cadbury while touring England to gather information for his great work on the "History and Antiquities of this Nation." Their hill, the villagers told him, was "Camallate, sumtyme a famose toun or castelle"; they had heard "say that Arture much resortid to Camalat." The top of the hill, where the circling ramparts of a centuries-old British hill fort could be traced beneath the grass, was known as Arthur's Palace, or so another antiquarian, William Camden, recorded when he visited Cadbury in Queen Elizabeth's day. Within less than an hour's walk were two villages named Queen's Camel and West Camel. On the banks of the Cam, a stream that wound through them, a great battle had been fought–the battle of Camlann, where Mordred had been slain and from which Arthur, grievously wounded, had been carried away to the Isle of Avalon at Glastonbury, only a few miles to the north across the low-lying Somerset basin.

These local traditions have long aroused the curiosity of antiquaries and archaeologists because they have an undeniable air of authenticity. The villages of Queen's Camel and West Camel are as real as South Cadbury itself; King Arthur's Causeway, which used to run across the marsh beneath the ramparts of the hill fort, can be traced in parts along the now well drained fields of the surrounding farms. The Cam still winds through the fields between them, and at the foot of the hill hurried burials did take place in the distant past, indicating that a battle had been fought there. Over the centuries ploughshares turning up the ground of the eighteen-acre field atop the summit uncovered a remarkable assortment of Roman coins, pottery, slingstones, building materials, and even traces of walls. It seemed that the hill, which had been occupied by Neolithic men more than three thousand years before the birth of Christ, still was inhabited at the time of the original Roman occupation of Britain. What the archaeologists and antiquarians did not know, however, was whether there ever had been an extensive reoccupation of the fort in the late fifth or early sixth century, the period in which Arthur must have lived.

When, in the 1890's, a party of antiquarians appeared on the hill to search for evidence of such a reoccupation, an old man came up to them and anxiously asked if they had come to take away the sleeping king from the hollow hill. What was found on that occasion is not recorded, but when a more scientific excavation was carried out shortly before World War I, several fragments of Romano-British pottery were uncovered, together with pieces of late Celtic workmanship. This was scarcely enough to establish a connection between South Cadbury Castle and Camelot.

In the 1950's, however, further discoveries were made, including pottery that dated from the Neolithic period and from the pre-Roman Iron Age. Most interesting of all from the Arthurian point of view, there also were pottery fragments that were similar to some already unearthed at the Early Christian monastery at Tintagel in Cornwall, as well as other shards of what may be a Merovingian glass bowl of a type imported from the Continent in the sixth century.

These important discoveries were identified by Dr. Ralegh Radford, a well-known Devonshire archaeologist, expert on Early Christian archaeology, and the most recent excavator of Glastonbury Abbey. Here was confirmation at last, Dr. Radford felt, "of the traditional identification of the site as the Camelot of Arthurian legend." Another whose interest was aroused was Geoffrey Ashe, author of a number of articles and books on the Arthurian period and legend. But without large sums of money, no proper excavation of the site could be undertaken, and the collection of sufficient funds to make a formal investigation of South Cadbury seemed unlikely until 1965, when Dr. Radford and Mr. Ashe finally succeeded in forming a Camelot Research Committee. The presidency of this committee was accepted by Sir Mortimer Wheeler, the world-famous excavator of Mohenjo Daro and the Indus civilizations of India, and the direction of the work was entrusted to Mr. Leslie Alcock, Reader in Archaeology at the University College of

South Wales. Newspapers and book publishers, the British Broadcasting Corporation, various learned societies, universities, and many private donors all gave financial help. The excavations were not to be limited to an effort to discover Camelot; they were to be devoted to unearthing all the secrets of the hill's history from its earliest known occupation by Neolithic man. Naturally, however, the chief interest focused upon the chances of finding actual archaeological proof of Arthur's having lived there.

These hopes were much increased by exciting finds that had been made at Glastonbury Tor, the strange, towering hill that rises so sharply above the ruins of the abbey. For here, in the early 1960's, a series of digs unearthed numerous fragments of sixth-century amphoras, imported from the Eastern Mediterranean, which once may have contained wine and oil, together with enough other clues to establish definitely that in the sixth century—Arthur's period—Glastonbury Tor must have been the site of the residence of some very important person.

Philip Rahtz, the director of excavations at Glastonbury, believes that at that time Glastonbury Tor may have been the stronghold of a local chieftain and perhaps served as a signal station of some kind. It could have been linked with South Cadbury Castle—the legendary

Camelot–to the south; with Brent Knoll, at the western end of the Mendip Hills, to the north; and from Brent Knoll still farther north across the mouth of the River Severn to another sixth-century British camp at Dinas Powys in South Wales. At least it is certain that when standing on Brent Knoll, one can see clearly both Cadbury Castle and Dinas Powys, which is a total distance of over forty miles. It also is likely that co-operation between the British on both sides of the Severn estuary was very close in the sixth century, with communications between them well co-ordinated. Not until the Battle of Dyrham in 577, some sixty years after Arthur's fight at Mount Badon, were the Saxons able to break through the line that connected the British defenders in Wales with those in the area of South Cadbury Castle.

Extensive digging at South Cadbury Castle began in the summer of 1966. The team of archaeologists and students who climbed the steep track to the summit of the hill, past King Arthur's Well, could not fail to hope that some astonishing discovery would be made that would establish Arthur's identity once and for all, incontrovertibly linking the hill with Camelot. On reaching the summit and looking down across the banks and ditches of the great ramparts that fall steeply away to the neat fields below, it certainly was possible to imagine, instead of those fields, the misty, haunted swamps that once were in their place and to picture Arthur riding out across the causeway to do battle against his enemies. For there is no doubt that to all but the most unimaginative minds, South Cadbury Castle is a strangely and strongly evocative place, at once both romantic and mysterious.

One young volunteer, who climbed the hill eagerly each morning from the school where she and most of the other student volunteers were lodged, said that every day she felt the same excitement; intuitively, she was convinced that here was Camelot. She felt sure that one day, as she and her friends knelt, scraping, in the trenches, or sat in the sunlight, washing the objects so carefully sieved from the soil, one day they would come across the longed-for incontrovertible proof.

But the digging that first year of 1966 revealed nothing so dramatic as a silver horse shoe or even a medallion bearing the vital, revealing legend ARTORIUS. Perhaps, it was unrealistic to hope for such clues; no coins minted in Britain in the sixth-century ever have been discovered anywhere. But quite a few inscriptions from this period have been found in Britain and Ireland, mostly incised on stone or metal. In Ireland and the Irish colonies in the west of Britain, these inscriptions are in Ogam, an alphabet of twenty letters, consisting of upright and sloping lines arranged in groups. In Britain, there are still some memorial slabs and pillars incised in the Roman fashion, although such memorials usually occur only in consecrated Early Christian cemeteries.

No inscriptions of any kind, however, turned up at South Cadbury in 1966. But the excavations, short as they were and preliminary as they were intended to be, did reveal much that was both important and illuminating.

Among other things, they revealed an extremely thick stone wall of late Saxon date, a wall that surely must have protected a fortified *burh*, or settlement. This lent weight to the belief that eleventh–century coins bearing the place mark CADANBYRIG, which have been discovered elsewhere, actually were made at a mint set up at South Cadbury. The excavations also revealed pieces of Roman armor; they revealed a pre-Roman Iron Age ditch and the remains of a collapsed Iron Age house; and from the Early Christian period between Roman times and the age of the English mint they brought to light enough shards of Mediterranean wine jars and dishes to suggest some sort of occupation in the sixth century.

This brief reconnaissance [concluded the report by Leslie Alcock, the expert who conducted it], covered less than one seven-hundredth part of the interior and has amply confirmed the rich potential of South Cadbury Castle in both structural and cultural terms. Particular interest attaches to the...long perspective of Celtic and Romano-British occupation which forms the chronological background to the Arthurian period at Cadbury. Clearly the site, in all its aspects, now demands large-scale exploration.

In the summer of 1967 excavations began again, after the Camelot Research Committee's appeal for funds had brought in further contributions from the original sponsors now joined by other newspapers, universities, and private people from all over England. That year some even more fascinating discoveries were made. For example, it definitely was established that the Saxon wall had a far more interesting history than previously had been supposed. Twenty-four feet of it was uncovered, displaying the longest stretch of Saxon wall yet seen in England. Beneath it was the last Iron Age rampart; and between the two was what the excavators called the Stony Bank.

The Stony Bank was found to contain yet another shard of imported sixth-century pottery, fragments of Roman-style roof tiles, lumps of tufa—a light stone used by the Romans in building construction—and a Roman slingstone. The slingstone's presence showed that this layer of the wall must have been built after the Roman conquest of Britain; the tiles and lumps of tufa probably came from a pagan temple built in the third or fourth century, when there was a pagan revival in Britain, and later demolished. The remains of such temples already had been discovered in the course of excavating several other Iron Age hill forts in Britain, and the existence of such a temple naturally was expected at Cadbury. The shard of pottery presumably got there after the Stony Bank was built and certainly before the Saxon wall was erected on top of it. Thanks to these discoveries, we can infer safely that Cadbury Castle was refortified in the sixth century as a stronghold against the Saxon invaders. Enthusiasts have built upon this the further inference that the castle must have been occupied by the type of princely warrior that Arthur is presumed to have been, but this is still supposition.

The digging out of the wall and of a new section of the summit was preceded by a geophysical survey. Instruments looking something like mine-detectors were taken over the ground to record readings that might indicate the pattern, shape, and density of the archaeological features beneath the turf. These instruments, which are known as soil conductivity meters and work on a principle similar to radar, had not been used in archaeological work before, and they were highly successful. The indications they gave of the pattern and density of post-holes and storage pits enabled Leslie Alcock, the director of excavations, to decide which were the most promising areas for that year's digging. When reduced to a printed plan, the readings revealed, by a series of dots in straight lines and in regular patterns, traces of what might have been extensive buildings constructed on top of the old Iron Age fortress in Arthur's time. One of the patterns looked remarkably like a main hall of some kind and aroused excitement among the workers.

The subsequent excavations did not reveal any more of this huge hall, but they did uncover something else of even greater interest. At first what was exposed baffled all the experts, and as the weeks of July and August, 1967, passed by, the problem seemed to grow still more incomprehensible. The diggers gradually unearthed, toward the western edge of the plot of land that had been marked out for examination, a trench that followed no explicable pattern.

None of the experts on the site could explain what possible purpose could have been served by digging a trench in such an apparently wayward manner. At first they thought that perhaps the hill had been used for military exercises during World War I. A notice board on which the volunteer diggers were asked to suggest their own interpretations of the mystery yielded such solutions as "A giraffe's tomb," or only slightly less improbably, "Patio of King Arthur's Palace."

Then, someone studying the lines of the trench, and imagining regular patterns that would incorporate the wedge-shaped segment in the northwestern corner, suddenly realized that if the U-shaped part of the pattern were to be repeated beneath the turf outside the area of excavation, what would emerge would be a cross.

A look at the dots on the geophysical survey plan showed that the pattern did, indeed, suggest that a cruciform trench might be unearthed in that sector of the plateau. No one, however, had been looking for such a shape. The team had been seeking evidence of the round buildings that had stood there in the Iron Age and of the rectangular buildings of the Early Christian period; and traces of these they had discovered. A building in the shape of an equal-armed cross had been so far removed from any expectations of the experts that the indications of its presence had totally escaped their detection.

In excited anticipation, Mr. Alcock gave orders for three trial digs outside the excavated area. In each case the diggers uncovered a further section of the expected trench, so that the cruciform plan was established. By deducing the rest of the pattern from what now was known of a part of it, the foundations of an entirely logical building appeared.

This design, it was suggested at once, could be explained most easily as the plan of a church. Such a plan, in the shape of an equal-armed Greek cross, appears to have been used first in the Middle East in the late fifth century. It was by no means common, however, in Arthur's time, even in the Mediterranean area. It has been suggested that this could have been Arthur's chapel at Camelot, a chapel that later was demolished by the Saxons to provide dressed stones for part of their massive stone wall. But no traces of mortar or chips of stone have been found in the trench to lend any confirmation to this attractive hypothesis, and it seems more likely that, for some reason that we never can know, work on the building was abandoned as soon as the excavations for its foundations had been dug.

Experts now question whether the trench was dug in the sixth century, or even by the Saxons. The latest suggestion is that this unfinished foundation may have been laid as late as the eleventh century and that perhaps building was broken off when the mint was removed and the rest of the Saxon settlement was abandoned early in the reign of King Canute. So far, no firm evidence has been found to back up any of these hypotheses. And without firm evidence, the archaeologist may conjecture all he likes, but he cannot make any definite pronouncement.

Digging at South Cadbury Castle was resumed in the summer of 1968, and soon further clues were unearthed. There were several more fragments–and unusually fine fragments–of sixth-century wine jars; traces of what may well prove to be the Saxon entrance to the strong-hold, the "gate of Camelot"; and part of the foundation trench for what seems to be a large, sixth-century hall cut into the bedrock of the plateau. Such a building, whose dimensions ten-tatively have been guessed as thirty-five feet in width and about seventy feet in length, may or may not have been the great hall of Camelot; but its discovery marks an exciting stage in the search for King Arthur's Britain, a search that still is continuing.

6

The Once and Future King

Even if the excavations at Camelot do not eventually uncover the reality of the Once and Future King, they already have helped to dispel the illusion that Arthur was the magical king of medieval romance. We can imagine him now, not as a knightly ruler clad in gleaming armor whose natural setting is the stone halls, parti-colored pavilions, and painted towers of medieval Camelot, but as a stern, rough warrior face to face with the brutal facts of sixth-century warfare, living in a stronghold built for defense rather than for pleasure.

He wears, not a silver breastplate, but a leather cuirass; not a plumed helmet, but a squat, close-fitting iron head-piece lined with leather; his breeches and boots also are of leather and colored brown like his belted tunic; his trousers are of coarse linen; his red woolen cloak, the only splash of color in an otherwise drab appearance, is fastened at his right shoulder with a bronze brooch of characteristic Celtic design; at his left side hangs a heavy iron sword in a leather scabbard; in his right hand he grasps the wooden shaft of a spear whose tip is of polished iron.

With this picture of Arthur in mind, it is possible to believe that, fanciful as the legends first appeared when we came across them in the pages of Malory, in each a kernel of truth lies concealed. Undeniably, the discovery of a truth buried deep within a legend is nothing new; and in this connection the story of the German archaeologist Heinrich Schliemann is very much to the point.

As a boy in the 1830's, Heinrich Schliemann was passionately fond of fairy stories, fables, and legends. In particular, he loved the epic stories of Homer's heroes, of Achilles and Hector, Paris and Helen, and the fabulous city of Troy, capital of King Priam, which after a ten-year siege by the Greeks was captured, burned and leveled. All his life, Schliemann remembered that his father, a pastor from the north German state of

Mecklenburg, had given him for a Christmas present when he was ten years old, a book on the main events of the Trojan War and the adventures of Odysseus; that he had decided then that when he was grown up, he would go to Troy and excavate the legendary city whose whereabouts no one knew.

Schliemann left school at fourteen and worked for five and a half years in a grocery store. Then he became an office boy in Amsterdam and spent his few moments of spare time studying foreign languages, working with such diligence that he achieved fluency in English, French, Dutch, Spanish, Italian, and Portuguese. He learned Russian in order to represent his firm in St. Petersburg, and he did so brilliantly there that before long he was in business on his own account as an import-export merchant. He was incredibly successful; by 1863, he had made so much money that he was able to retire, at the age of forty-one, and devote himself to the studies that had fascinated him for so long.

In 1868 he sailed for Greece, determined to prove wrong the scholars and experts who had relegated the Trojan epic to the world of myth. He was as convinced in late middle age as he had been as a boy that the Greece of Homer's *Iliad* once really had existed, that Achilles and Agamemnon, Hector and Aeneas, were actual historical heroes who had lived and fought and died. Again and again Schliemann read the *Iliad*, searching for clues that would lead him to Troy, the great city that so many scholars said never had existed, following Homer's directions as best he could. His trail led him to Hissarlik, a small town in western Turkey, a few miles from the southern entrance to the Dardanelles. There, with a millionaire's resources to indulge his whim, Schliemann set a hundred men to work digging for months on end, ignoring ridicule and discomfort alike. And there he uncovered not only the ruins of King Priam's city, but also the traces of a whole vanished civilization previously unknown to archaeology.

Schliemann's faith and ability found Troy and proved that a legend can have its base in historical reality. So may it be some day with Camelot and the facts behind the Arthurian legend. An English writer, Beram Saklatvala, recently has made several ingenious suggestions to account for some of the legend's varied details. He has guessed, for instance, that the source of the French book from which Malory claimed he had taken the story of the sword in the stone might have been a now lost Latin chronicle in which some such sentence as this occurred: "*Arthur gladium ex saxo eripuit*"–"Arthur drew, or seized, a sword from the stone." This remarkable feat, so Malory tells us, was beyond the power of other men and thus proved Arthur's right to be king. This was the kind of fantastic story that induced the printer Caxton to tell his readers that they were "at liberty to believe" that the *Morte d'Arthur* was not all true. But Saklatvala suggests, could the Latin phrase be a mistaken copy of the record of an authentic fact?

The words that arouse disbelief are *ex saxo*, "from a stone." Medieval clerks were in the habit of omitting the letter *n* and of showing the omission by a stroke drawn in above the next letter, so that *ex saxoe*, or *ex saxone*, would mean that Arthur took the sword from the Saxon rather than from the stone, a very different and wholly credible event. Whether we are to interpret it that Arthur struck the sword from the hand of a particular and much-feared Saxon warrior in single combat, or that the Saxon is intended to mean the whole Saxon race whose ambitions were thwarted at Mount Badon, it is not difficult to believe that such a victory would ensure for Arthur the leadership of the British armies, if not indeed the throne of the surviving British kingdom in the West Country.

The story of the other sword in the legend, Excalibur, may have passed into the realm of myth by a similar process, Saklatvala believes. In Malory's version of the tale the sword appears in the midst of a lake of "fair water and broad," and after the battle of Camlann, when Arthur instructs Sir Bedivere to return it to the waters, "there came an arm above the water and met it, and caught it, and so shook it thrice and brandished, and then vanished away the hand with the sword in the water." Geoffrey of Monmouth also writes of Arthur's "peerless sword, forged in the Isle of Avalon," which he calls Caliburn.

Saklatvala suggests that there might have been an early chronicle in which Arthur was said to have obtained his sword *ex cale burno* from beside the river Cale, in which case its name and its connection with water would be readily explained. It is indeed a fact that the Romans ascribed some of the merits of their iron swords to the quality of the water into which the blacksmith plunged the heated blades in order to temper them by sudden cooling. It is also a fact that there is a river Cale within an hour's ride of South Cadbury Castle.

Unfortunately, eminent scholars have refuted Saklatvala's thesis. Apart from the fact that the medieval Latin word *burna*, "stream," is recorded for the first time only about 1135, the period in which Geoffrey actually was completing his *History*, the Somersetshire river Cale in his day was written *Cawel*, and the spelling "Cale" does not appear until Elizabethan days. There is also doubt about whether the *ex* in Excalibur stands for the Latin word meaning "out of"; it probably is just a prefix used to accentuate the first syllable in the Old French form of the word "escalibor"—an accentuation rather like that in "especial," compared with "special," for instance.

The generally accepted derivation of the name of Arthur's sword, according to the distinguished Arthurian scholar R. S. Loomis, is Celtic rather than Latin. Excalibur's name in the Welsh romances is Caledvwlch, apparently based on the Welsh words *calet*, "hard," and *bwlch*, "notch." Professor Loomis believed, however, that this was just a Welsh approximation of the name of another famous sword, renowned in Irish legends: Caladcolg, or Caladbolg, meaning "Hard Sword" or "Hard Sheath," which was made by the fairies for an Ulster hero named Fergus. In one of these Irish sagas the hero Fergus Mac Leite uses Caladcolg to do battle with a lake monster. Victorious, but mortally wounded, he begs his followers to give his sword only to another hero named Fergus and to treasure it "that none other take it from you; my share of the matter for all time shall be this: that men shall rehearse the story of the sword." There are some obvious parallels here with the story of Arthur as we know it from Malory, although no scholar has done more than point out the similarities.

The fact that the quest for Excalibur's true source leads back to Celtic myth and legend should not disappoint us unduly. It was natural that the defeated British people should glorify the memory of their greatest hero with legendary attributes that originally belonged to other heroes, or even to the gods of their pagan past. As Professor Loomis has put it:

> Throughout the world's history, clouds of legend have gathered about the heads of military leaders who have caught the imagination of a people. This happened to Alexander and Charlemagne, to Napoleon and Washington. For the Britons it was enough that Arthur inflicted a series of defeats on their heathen foes and staved off for a time their expulsion from what was to be England...To this racial hero the Welsh and to some extent the Cornish attached a floating mass of native traditions, together with matter derived from Ireland and the Britons of the North. This they passed on to the Bretons, who shared their passionate devotion to the memory of Arthur, and the Bretons in turn, speaking French, were able by the fire and the charm of their recitals to captivate the imagination of the non-Celtic peoples. Thus the obscure battle leader of a defeated race became the champion of all Christendom, his knights paragons of valor and chivalry, and the ladies of his court nonpareils of beauty...

There is actually no need to find historical parallels in order to believe in the historicity of Arthur, nor is it necessary to identify the Round Table with the war council of Arthur's cavalry commanders in order to believe that there were such commanders. We may believe nothing else in *Le Morte d 'Arthur,* but of the existence of its central figure we scarcely can be in doubt. We even may believe, as one historian has said of the Glastonbury stories, that none of the Arthurian legends bears any relation to records of facts, but the existence of those legends is in itself a very great fact.

And who can say that even now, after fourteen hundred years, some vital evidence will not be found to blow away the mists of legend and reveal in sudden clarity an undeniable truth? In the meantime, we can draw together a tentative biography of Arthur based upon the few facts we possess and the deductions that can be made from those facts.

He was born about 475 into a well-to-do West Country family and given a Roman name, Artorius, in token of the family's traditional loyalty to the empire. As a young man in the Christian kingdom of Ambrosius, the last outpost of Roman influence in Britain, he showed powers of leadership that led to his taking over

the defense of the kingdom on Ambrosius'
death. He formed and trained an effective force
of mobile cavalry, which fought as a reliable, disciplined unit in the traditional Roman style. He
persuaded most of the British kings to accept
him as their supreme war leader, a Count of
Britain on the Roman model, and to appoint
him commander of their local levies.

With his own cavalry and what support he
could pick up on his way, he ranged far and
wide over the island, attacking its heathen invaders in campaigns that took him from Chester
in the west to the forests of Caledonia north
of Hadrian's Wall and into the lands occupied
by the East Saxons and the North Angles. He
succeeded in giving his cause a Christian and
Catholic flavor by invoking the protection of
the Virgin Mary, yet he offended the Church
by the impositions he was forced to make upon
the monasteries in order to obtain the supplies
he needed to carry on the fight against the
pagans.

In 516 his enemies converged upon his
defenses in the southwest, but at Mount Badon,
somewhere near the Wansdyke, he led his cavalry triumphantly against them, inflicting such
an overwhelming defeat that peace reigned for
a generation. It was broken by a civil war in
which Arthur and Mordred, the illegitimate son

who sought to replace him, both were killed.
For some twenty years, however, Arthur had
been the recognized master of all those parts of
Britain not occupied by the Angles and Saxons.
He was proclaimed king by his troops, and he
held with his knights, or companions, a kind
of court that later generations were to know
as Camelot.

Once again, facts and speculations merge into
myth, and we are left searching for that incontest-
able proof that some day may solve the riddle of
Malory's "great conqueror and excellent King"
whose story has been written anew generation
after generation. To each he has had a different
aspect; to one, he is a tyrant king; to another, a
mighty warrior; to yet another, a fairy ruler of
a magical subterranean kingdom; to Malory, he
is a knightly hero, noble and tragic, and it is this
image of Arthur that probably has left the most
lasting impression.

Yet even while Malory wrote, the temper of
the times had changed. The world he described
still had its appeal, even to the aggressive monarch Henry VIII, who boasted of his descent
from Arthur (through the Welsh princes to
whom the Tudor family were distantly related)
and enjoyed jousts, tournaments, and splendid
events of all kinds. But Henry was no pattern
of knightly behavior, and in the upsurge of

interest in Classical literature and art and the clash between Protestant and Catholic faiths that characterized the sixteenth century, the whole idea of medieval chivalry began to seem an anachronism. It was not just that new weapons had rendered knights obsolete; the Elizabethans, practical and realistic men that they were, tended to see them in terms of Cervantes' Don Quixote, insanely tilting at windmills. The unreal world of Malory's stories was replaced by the discovery of a New World, unexplored and enchanting. Who could interest himself in the fancies of Arthur's imaginary court at Camelot when Florida and Santiago beckoned the adventurous, when men could read of Drake's circumnavigation of their own globe?

Some Elizabethans could—among, them Edmund Spenser, whose *Faerie Queene*, published just before the sixteenth century drew to its close, triumphantly combines the new influences of the Renaissance with the antique legends of Britain. Spenser died without completing his great work, but in a letter to Sir Walter Raleigh, written in 1589, he described his intentions: "to fashion a gentleman or noble person in vertuous and gentle discipline. Which for that I conceived should be the most plausible and pleasing…I chose the historie of king Arthure, as most fit for the excellencie of his person, beeing made famous by many mens former workes, and also furthest from the danger of envie, and suspicion of present time." Following the style of Homer, Vergil, and the Italian poets Ariosto and Tasso, Spenser goes on, he has labored to portray in Arthur "before he was king, the image of a brave knight, perfected in the twelve private morall vertues, as Aristotle hath devised."

Despite Spenser's intention of making Arthur his hero, the prince is more of an incidental figure in the six books that are all we have of the *Faerie Queene*. He meets the various knights and ladies as they go about their adventures but plays no definite part in them. Spenser uses much material from Geoffrey of Monmouth's *History*, adapting or altering it freely to suit his own poetic purpose. In this sense, he is treating Arthur as a purely legendary figure rather than an historical one, an attitude that foreshadows the disillusionment that the writers of the following century were to feel most strongly.

"Charles James Stuart/Claims Arthur's Seat" was the anagram current at the coronation of James I in 1603. As the Stuart king of Scotland mounted the throne of England, the poets boasted that the prophecies of Merlin were fulfilled now that the island of Britain was united under one crown. Ben Jonson and

Thomas Campion wrote masques and pageants celebrating James' accession; Jonson planned an Arthurian epic of his own. As the new monarch entered London, a complicated double British pedigree, claiming James' direct descent from Arthur on both sides of his family, was displayed on two seventy-foot pyramids at the entrance to the Strand.

But the new golden age was a short one. James and his son, Charles I, believed that they were divinely appointed to rule; Parliament, increasing in strength, grew ever more rebellious. The Stuart kings were poor representatives of the royal state, and champions of Parliament and the English constitution began to pour scorn on their ancestor, King Arthur, and look instead to Arthur's ancient enemies, the Anglo-Saxons, as the real fathers of the country, its language and its laws. Geoffrey of Monmouth's *History* was ridiculed; he had "stuft himselfe with infinit Fables and grosse absurdities," scoffed one Parliamentary sympathizer.

Milton, the greatest poet of the age, had been fascinated as an undergraduate by Italian romances, and strongly influenced by Spenser, planned an epic poem on "the kings of my native land, and Arthur, who carried war even into fairyland." Later, as a stanch Puritan and supporter of Parliament in its battles with the

Crown, he not only abandoned Arthur as a fit subject for an epic but also, in his *History of Britain*, made every attempt to discredit the British hero, calling him "more renown'd in Songs and Romances, than in True stories." Nennius he dismisses as "a very trivial writer," and after a discussion of the Battle of Mount Badon, Milton the historian sums up: "But who Arthur was, and whether ever any such reign'd in *Britan*, hath bin doubted heertofore, and may again with good reason."

But after the Civil War and the bleak rule of Oliver Cromwell came the Restoration of Charles II in 1660, and the first new book on Arthur in many decades, a retelling of the "Most Famous History of that Most Renowned Christian Worthy Arthur King of the Britaines, and his famous knights of the Round Table," welcomed the new king home from exile. The wheel began to turn once more, as poets and playwrights returned to the abandoned theme. John Dryden, a loyalist, wanted to produce an Arthurian epic poem that would popularize the idea of Stuart rule but was too busy writing plays to spare the time to compose it. In 1691, however, he did use the subject as an opera, *King Arthur*, for which Henry Purcell supplied the music. This concentrates chiefly on Arthur's battles with the Saxons and makes Arthur and a Saxon prince Oswald rivals for the love of Emmeline, the blind daughter of the Duke of Cornwall. Arthur, naturally, wins his bride, whose sight is conveniently restored by some magic drops provided by Merlin.

It is ironic that although the three greatest poets of the seventeenth century, Jonson, Milton, and Dryden, all planned epic poems on the subject of Arthur, they did not write them. Two massive Arthurian epics were composed, however, by King William III's Physician in Ordinary, Sir Richard Blackmore, who found the writing of epics "an Innocent Amusement to entertain me in such leisure hours which were usually past away before in Conversation and unprofitable hearing and telling of News." He would have done better to confine himself to the news, however unprofitable; he and his epics are known today only because a far better poet, Alexander Pope, labeled him "the everlasting Blackmore" who "sings so loudly and who sings so long."

The eighteenth century saw little interest in Arthur; it was an age of reason and of practicality. Merlin already had become a figure of fun; astrologers used his head as a sign outside their fortune-telling establishments. The popular tale of Tom Thumb made the tiny man a knight at King Arthur's court, in love with the king's daughter Princess Hunca Munca. It was not until the end of the century that a rekindled interest in the Middle Ages brought Romantic poets and painters once again to the Arthurian cycle. Early in the nineteenth century Walter Scott and Robert Southey wrote on Arthurian subjects and planned or edited new versions of Malory. By the middle of the century, medievalism was a passion, reflected in the Gothic art and architecture of Victorian England. Edward Bulwer-Lytton, William Morris and the Pre-Raphaelite Brotherhood of artists and writers, Matthew Arnold, and various lesser poets turned their attention in turn to the Arthurian theme. And in 1859 Alfred Tennyson published the first series of the *Idylls of the King*, which translated Malory's characters and their acts into a gospel for Victorian times.

Tennyson had had this project in mind for many years. He had made visits to places traditionally associated with King Arthur in the West Country, seeking material and impressions. He had read and reread the *Morte d'Arthur*, and he had some knowledge, too, of the French and Norman chronicles and of the heroic legends of Wales. His first Arthurian poem, *The Lady of Shalott*, was published in 1832, when he was only twenty-three; he already, was planning fragments and themes for an epic of some kind on what he called "the greatest of all poetic subjects." But he was preoccupied by other work and uncertain of exactly what shape his epic should take. By the 1850's, he had found the ideal narrative form for what was to become his lifework: a series of long, linked parts that covered the full sequence of the story from Arthur's mysterious birth to his disappearance into the mists of Avalon.

Publication of the first four idylls in 1859 was greeted with unparalleled enthusiasm. Ten thousand copies of the work were sold within the first week, and Tennyson was offered five thousand guineas for another volume of the same length. Over the next twenty-five years he added further idylls of Arthur, his knights, and the ladies of his court, and even when the series of twelve was complete, the poet continued to work with it, altering lines to make his meaning clearer, to within a year of his death in 1892. The public was enraptured; the publishers had to contend with orders for forty thousand copies even before publication. In homes all over the English-speaking world his hauntingly beautiful verses were committed to memory.

Tennyson's King Arthur, a "blameless King" of the utmost moral rectitude, is far removed from Malory's passionate knight. In the *Idylls* there is none of the open sexuality that pervades Malory's Camelot. Just as Geoffrey of Monmouth's Arthur was called into being in Stephen's time to give a heroic British origin to the newly established Norman kingdom, Tennyson's Arthur reflects the sentiments and morality admired by the current representatives of the English monarchy, Queen Victoria and her consort, Prince Albert. The poet depicts Britain of Arthur's day not as an ideal period, but as a kind of analogy from which Victorian readers could draw parallels for their own time. He wanted to stress virtues that seemed to him excellent, idealism, chivalry, unselfish patriotism, and religious faith, and to show that even the finest and greatest ideals often go down in defeat, as Arthur's did. In the end, however, his message is one of hope, as Bedivere, despairing, calls the "true old times...dead,/When every morning brought a noble chance,/And every chance brought out a noble knight."

And slowly answer'd Arthur from the barge:
"The old order changeth, yielding place to new,
And God fulfils himself in many ways,
Lest one good custom should corrupt the world.
Comfort thyself: what comfort is in me?
I have lived my life, and that which I have done
May He within Himself make pure! but thou,
If thou shouldst never see my face again,

Pray for my soul. More things are wrought by prayer

Than this world dreams of…"

The high idealism of Tennyson's Arthur has been seen as a direct reflection of the virtues of Prince Albert, to whom, after his premature death in 1861, Tennyson dedicated the Idylls: "These to His Memory–since he held them dear,/Perchance as finding there unconsciously/ Some image of himself…" The dedication certainly makes of the epic a public compliment to the rulers whose Poet Laureate Tennyson was; but his purpose went deeper than that. The characters are symbolic: Arthur represents the ideal soul, which struggles to fulfill itself in the world of sense (represented by marriage with Guinevere), while the Round Table stands for the soul's attempt to ennoble and control human emotions–an ideal that gradually is corrupted and eroded by the sin of Lancelot and Guinevere. But as Tennyson himself put it: "Every reader must find his own interpretation according to his ability, and according to his sympathy with the poet."

The influence of Arthurian legend upon the art and literature of the period continued unabated; even the new craft of photography was employed to make a series of illustrations of Tennyson's *Idylls*, while some of the finest artists of the day contributed their own visions of Arthur's romantic and elusive world. Musicians, too, were drawn to the story of Arthur, notably the German composer Richard Wagner, who had produced the first of his Arthurian music-dramas, *Lohengrin*, in 1850 and followed it with the famous *Tristan und Isolde* in 1865 and in 1882 with *Parsifal*, based upon the German legends of Percival and the quest for the Holy Grail. To ensure the total unity that he demanded, Wagner wrote both words and music for his great operas, and the regular performance of his works at the Bayreuth festivals and their immediate and overwhelming popularity formed yet another current in the extraordinary spread of Arthurian influences.

In our own day the concept of knighthood has been celebrated anew. T. H. White's delightful books about King Arthur, which he gathered together under the title of *The Once and Future King*, have brought the legend to life for a new generation, both by themselves and through *Camelot*, the musical and the film based upon them.

White presents the story in a fresh and vivid light, filling it with humor and magic, with lessons in hawking and boar-hunting, in archery and jousting, in history and animal lore. But he treats his material with the same loving respect

with which Sir Thomas Malory treated it, and
at the end of the last book White actually brings
Malory himself into the story, as a page with a
face expressive of youth's innocence and certainty. Arthur, tired and soon to die, tells the
boy what the purpose of his life has been and
urges him not to fight in the final battle with
Mordred on the following day but to take horse
to Warwickshire, there to think of himself as
a kind of vessel to carry on the idea of the
Round Table and spread its message to future
generations.

Put it like this [Arthur says to him]. There was a king once,
called King Arthur. That is me. When he came to the throne
of England, he found that all the kings and barons were
fighting against each other like madmen... They did a lot of
bad things, because they lived by force. Now this king had
an idea, and the idea was that force ought to be used, if it
were used at all, on behalf of justice, not on its own account.
Follow this, young boy. He thought that if he could get his
barons fighting for truth, and to help weak people, and to
redress wrongs, then their fighting might not be such a bad
thing as once it used to be. So he gathered together all the
true and kindly people that he knew, and he dressed them
in armour, and he made them knights, and taught them
his idea, and set them down, at a Round Table. And King
Arthur loved his Table with all his heart. He was prouder of
it than he was of his own dear wife, and for many years his

new knights went about killing ogres, and rescuing damsels and saving poor prisoners, and trying to set the world to rights. That was the King's idea.

And that, to White, was all that really mattered. He was not concerned with the "real" Arthur; he turned history upside down to recreate a medieval knight at odds with the ways of a violent world. He despised those historians and archaeologists who were trying to track a beautiful legend to its source and thus, in his view, destroy its beauty. For him Arthur was "not a distressed Briton hopping about in a suit of woad in the fifth century," but a true knight with "an open face, with kind eyes and a reliable or faithful expression, as though he was a good learner who enjoyed being alive…He had never been unjustly treated, for one thing, so he was kind to other people."

More than a thousand years separates White's King Arthur and Nennius' Commander in the Battles, but perhaps they were not such different people, after all. No one ever will know. But the quest for Arthur of Britain never can destroy the beauty of the works that his legend has inspired or the fascination of the legend itself. Since Arthur's nobility and valor first inspired the hearts of his followers, his story has dignified the human spirit. The search for the man himself has become a continuing quest for what lies hidden in the hearts of all men, and it may lead us one day to the truth about the Once and Future King.

Acknowledgments

The Editors are particularly grateful for the assistance of Mrs. Christine Sutherland in London. In addition, they would like to thank the following individuals and organizations:

W. H. Allen Publishers, London
Mr. Geoffrey Ashe
Mrs. Susan Bakker
Bibliothèque de l' Arsenal, Paris–M. Jacques Guignard
Bibliothèque Municipale de Douai–Mme. Y. Duhamel
Bibliothèque Nationale, Paris–M. Marcel Thomas; Mme. Le Monnier

The quotation on p.128 is from *Arthurian Tradition and Chrétien de Troyes*, by Roger Sherman Loomis, published by Columbia University

Press, 1949. The quotation on pp.142-3 is from *The Once and Future King*, © 1939, 1940, and 1958 by T. H. White, reprinted by permission of G. P. Putnam's Sons.

TEMPUS – REVEALING HISTORY

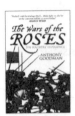

The Wars of the Roses
The Soldiers' Experience
ANTHONY GOODMAN
'A fascinating book' *TLS*

£12.99

0 7524 3731 3

The Vikings
MAGNUS MAGUNSSON
'Serious, engaging history'
BBC History Magazine

£9.99

0 7524 2699 0

William the Conqueror
DAVID BATES
'As expertly woven as the Bayeux Tapestry'
BBC History Magazine

£12.99

0 7524 2960 4

Agincourt: A New History
ANNE CURRY
'A *tour de force*' **Alison Weir**
'*The* book on the battle' **Richard Holmes**
A ***BBC History Magazine*** book of the year 2005

£12.99

0 7524 2828 4

Hereward The Last Englishman
PETER REX
'An enthralling work of historical detection'
Robert Lacey

£17.99

0 7524 3318 0

The English Resistance
The Underground War Against the Normans
PETER REX
'An invaluable rehabilitation of an ignored
resistance movement' ***The Sunday Times***

£12.99

0 7524 3733 X

Richard III
MICHAEL HICKS
'A most important book by the greatest living
expert on Richard' ***Desmond Seward***

£9.99

0 7524 2589 7

The Peasants' Revolt
England's Failed Revolution of 1381
ALASTAIR DUNN
'A stunningly good book... totally absorbing'
Melvyn Bragg

£9.99

0 7524 2965 5

If you are interested in purchasing other books published by Tempus, or in case you have difficulty finding
any Tempus books in your local bookshop, you can also place orders directly through our website:
www.tempus-publishing.com

TEMPUS REVEALING HISTORY

Scotland
From Prehistory to the Present
FIONA WATSON
***The Scotsman* Bestseller**
£9.99

0 7524 2591 9

1314 Bannockburn
ARYEH NUSBACHER
'Written with good-humoured verve as
befits a rattling "yarn of sex, violence and
terror"'
History Scotland
£9.99

0 7524 2982 5

Flodden
NIALL BARR
'Tells the story brilliantly'
The Sunday Post
£9.99

0 7524 2593 5

Scotland's Black Death
The Foul Death of the English
KAREN JILLINGS
'So incongruously enjoyable a read, and so
attractively presented by the publishers'
The Scotsman
£12.99

978 07524 3732 3

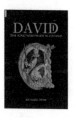

David I The King Who Made Scotland
RICHARD ORAM
'Enthralling... sets just the right tone as the
launch-volume of an important new series
of royal biographies' ***Magnus Magnusson***
£17.99

0 7524 2825 X

The Kings & Queens of Scotland
RICHARD ORAM
'A serious, readable work that sweeps across
a vast historical landscape' ***The Daily Mail***
£12.99

0 7524 3814 X

The Second Scottish Wars of Independence 1332–1363
CHRIS BROWN
'Explodes the myth of the invincible Bruces...
lucid and highly readable' ***History Scotland***
£12.99

0 7524 3812 3

Robert the Bruce: A Life Chronicled
CHRIS BROWN
'A masterpiece of research'
The Scots Magazine
£30

0 7524 2575 7

If you are interested in purchasing other books published by Tempus, or in case you have difficulty finding any Tempus
books in your local bookshop, you can also place orders directly through our website

www.tempus-publishing.com

TEMPUS REVEALING HISTORY

William Wallace
The True Story of Braveheart
CHRIS BROWN
'The truth about Braveheart' *The Scottish Daily Mail*
£17.99
0 7524 3432 2

An Abundance of Witches
The Great Scottish Witch-Hunt
P.G. MAXWELL-STUART
'An amazing account of Scots women in league with the Devil' *The Sunday Post*
£17.99
0 7524 3329 6

The Roman Conquest of Scotland
The Battle of Mons Graupius AD 84
JAMES E. FRASER
'Challenges a long held view' *The Scottish Sunday Express*
£17.99
0 7524 3325 3

Scottish Voices from the Great War
DEREK YOUNG
'A treasure trove of personal letters and diaries from the archives'
   Trevor Royle
£17.99
0 7524 3326 1

Culloden
The Last Charge of the Highland Clans
JOHN SADLER
£25
0 7524 3955 3

The Scottish Civil War
The Bruces & the Balliols & the War for the Control of Scotland
MICHAEL PENMAN
'A highly informative and engaging account' *Historic Scotland*
£16.99
0 7524 2319 3

The Pictish Conquest
The Battle of Dunnichen 685 & the Birth of Scotland
JAMES E. FRASER
£12.99

Scottish Voices from the Second World War
DEREK YOUNG
'Poignant memories of a lost generation… heart-rending' *The Sunday Post*
£17.99
0 7524 3710 0

If you are interested in purchasing other books published by Tempus, or in case you have difficulty finding any Tempus books in your local bookshop, you can also place orders directly through our website

www.tempus-publishing.com

TEMPUS – REVEALING HISTORY

Private 12768 Memoir of a Tommy
JOHN JACKSON

'Unique... a beautifully written, strikingly honest account of a young man's experience of combat' *Saul David*

'At last we have John Jackson's intensely personal and heartfelt little book to remind us there was a view of the Great War other than Wilfred Owen's' *The Daily Mail*

£9.99   0 7524 3531 0

The German Offensives of 1918
MARTIN KITCHEN

'A lucid, powerfully driven narrative' *Malcolm Brown*
'Comprehensive and authoritative... first class' *Holger H. Herwig*

£13.99   0 7524 3527 2

Verdun 1916
MALCOLM BROWN

'A haunting book which gets closer than any other to that wasteland marked by death' *Richard Holmes*

£9.99   0 7524 2599 4

The Forgotten Front
The East African Campaign 1914–1918
ROSS ANDERSON

'Excellent... fills a yawning gap in the historical record'
The Times Literary Supplement
'Compelling and authoritative'
Hew Strachan

£12.99   978 07524 4126 9

Agincourt
A New History
ANNE CURRY

'A highly distinguished and convincing account' *Christopher Hibbert*
'A *tour de force*' *Alison Weir*
'*The* book on the battle' *Richard Holmes*
A *BBC History Magazine* Book of the Year 2005

£12.99   978 07524 3813 1

The Welsh Wars of Independence
DAVID MOORE

'Beautifully written, subtle and remarkably perceptive' *John Davies*

£12.99   978 07524 4128 3

Bosworth 1485 Psychology of a Battle
MICHAEL K. JONES

'Most exciting... a remarkable tale' *The Guardian*
'Insightful and rich study of the Battle of Bosworth... no longer need Richard play the villain' *The Times Literary Supplement*

£12.99   0 7524 2594 3

The Battle of Hastings 1066
M.K. LAWSON

'Blows away many fundamental assumptions about the battle of Hastings... an exciting and indispensable read' *David Bates*
A *BBC History Magazine* Book of the Year 2003

£12.99   978 07524 4177 1

TEMPUS – REVEALING HISTORY

Freaks
JAN BONDESON

'Reveals how these tragic individuals triumphed over their terrible adversity' **The Daily Mail**
'Well written and superbly illustrated'
The Financial Times

£9.99   0 7524 3662 7

Bollywood
MIHIR BOSE

'Pure entertainment' **The Observer**
'Insightful and often hilarious' **The Sunday Times**
'Gripping' **The Daily Telegraph**

£9.99   978 07524 4382 9

King Arthur
CHRISTOPHER HIBBERT

'A pearl of biographers' **New Statesman**

£12.99   978 07524 3933 4

Arnhem
William Buckingham

'Reveals the reason why the daring attack failed'
The Daily Express

£10.99   0 7524 3187 0

Cleopatra
PATRICIA SOUTHERN

'In the absence of Cleopatra's memoirs Patricia Southern's commendably balanced biography will do very well'
The Sunday Telegraph

£9.99   978 07524 4336 2

The Prince In The Tower
MICHAEL HICKS

'The first time in ages that a publisher has sent me a book I actually want to read' **David Starkey**

£9.99   978 07524 4386 7

The Battle of Hastings 1066
M. K. LAWSON

'A **BBC History Magazine** book of the year 2003
'The definitive book on this famous battle'
The Journal of Military History

£12.99   978 07524 4177 1

Loos 1915
NICK LLOYD

'A revealing new account based on meticulous documentary research' **Corelli Barnett**
'Should fiinaly consign Alan Clark's Farrago, The Donkeys, to the waste paperbasket'
Hew Strachan
'Plugs a yawning gap in the existing literature... this book will set the agenda for debate of the battle for years to come' **Gary Sheffield**

£25   0 7524 3937 5

If you are interested in purchasing other books published by Tempus, or in case you have difficulty finding any Tempus books in your local bookshop, you can also place orders directly through our website

www.tempus-publishing.com

TEMPUS – REVEALING HISTORY

The Defence and Fall of Singapore
1940-42
BRIAN FARRELL

'A multi-pronged attack on those who made the defence of Malaya and Singapore their duty... [an] exhaustive account of the clash between Japanese and British Empire forces' **BBC History Magazine**

'An original and provocative new history of the battle' *Hew Strachan*

£13.99   0 7524 3768 2

Zulu!
The Battle for Rorke's Drift 1879
EDMUND YORKE

'A clear, detailed exposition... a very good read' ***Journal of the Royal United Service Institute for Defence Studies***

£12.99   0 7524 3502 7

Paras
The Birth of British Airborne Forces from Churchill's Raiders to 1st Parachute Brigade
WILLIAM F. BUCKINGHAM

£17.99   0 7524 3530 2

Voices from the Trenches
Life & Death on the Western Front
ANDY SIMPSON AND TOM DONOVAN

'A vivid picture of life on the Western Front... compelling reading' ***The Daily Telegraph***

'Offers the reader a wealth of fine writing by soldiers of the Great War whose slim volumes were published so long ago or under such obscure imprints that they have all but disappeared from sight like paintings lost under the grime of ages' *Malcolm Brown*

£12.99   0 7524 3905 7

Loos 1915
NICK LLOYD

'A revealing new account based on meticulous documentary research... I warmly commend this book to all who are interested in history and the Great War' *Corelli Barnett*

'Should finally consign Alan Clarke's farrago, *The Donkeys*, to the waste paper basket' *Hew Strachan*

£25   0 7524 3937 5

The Last Nazis
SS Werewolf Guerilla Resistance in Europe 1944-47
PERRY BIDDISCOMBE

'Detailed, meticulously researched and highly readable... a must for all interested in the end of the Second World War' *Military Illustrated*

£12.99   0 7524 2342 8

Omaha Beach A Flawed Victory
ADRIAN LEWIS

'A damning book' **BBC History Magazine**

£12.99   0 7524 2975 2

The English Civil War
A Historical Companion
MARTYN BENNETT

'Martyn Bennett knows more about the nuts and bolts of the English Civil War than anybody else alive' *Ronald Hutton*

'A most useful and entertaining book – giving us all precise detail about the events, the places, the people and the things that we half-know about the civil war and many more things that we did not know at all' *John Morrill*

£25   0 7524 3186 2

If you are interested in purchasing other books published by Tempus, or in case you have difficulty finding any Tempus books in your local bookshop, you can also place orders directly through our website

www.tempus-publishing.com

TEMPUS – REVEALING HISTORY

R.J.Mitchell
Schooldays to Spitfire
GORDON MITCHELL
'[A] readable and poignant story'
The Sunday Telegraph

£12.99   0 7524 3727 5

Forgotten Soldiers of the First World War
Lost Voices from the Middle Eastern Front
DAVID WOODWARD
'A brilliant new book of hitherto unheard voices from a haunting theatre of the First World War' *Malcolm Brown*

£12.99   978 07524 4307 2

1690 Battle of the Boyne
PÁDRAIG LENIHAN
'An almost impeccably impartial account of the most controversial military engagement in British history' *The Daily Mail*

£12.99   0 7524 3304 0

Hell at the Front
Combat Voices from the First World War
TOM DONOVAN
'Fifty powerful personal accounts, each vividly portraying the brutalising reality of the Great War... a remarkable book' *Max Arthur*

£12.99   0 7524 3940 5

Amiens 1918
JAMES MCWILLIAMS & R. JAMES STEEL
'A masterly portrayal of this pivotal battle'
Soldier: The Magazine of the British Army

£25   0 7524 2860 8

Before Stalingrad
Hitler's Invasion of Russia 1941
DAVID GLANTZ
'Another fine addition to Hew Strachan's excellent *Battles and Campaigns* series'
BBC History Magazine

£9.99   0 7524 2692 3

The SS
A History 1919-45
ROBERT LEWIS KOEHL
'Reveals the role of the SS in the mass murder of the Jews, homosexuals and gypsies and its organisation of death squads throughout occupied Europe' *The Sunday Telegraph*

£9.99   0 7524 2559 5

Arnhem 1944
WILLIAM BUCKINGHAM
'Reveals the real reason why the daring attack failed' *The Daily Express*

£10.99   0 7524 3187 0

If you are interested in purchasing other books published by Tempus, or in case you have difficulty finding any Tempus books in your local bookshop, you can also place orders directly through our website

www.tempus-publishing.com

TEMPUS – REVEALING HISTORY

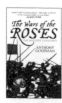

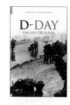

The Wars of the Roses
The Soldiers' Experience
ANTHONY GOODMAN
'Sheds light on the lot of the common soldier as never before' *Alison Weir*
'A meticulous work'
The Times Literary Supplement

£12.99   0 7524 3731 3

D-Day
The First 72 Hours
WILLIAM F. BUCKINGHAM
'A compelling narrative' *The Observer*
A *BBC History Magazine* Book of the Year 2004

£9.99   0 7524 2842 2

English Battlefields
500 Battlefields that Shaped English History
MICHAEL RAYNER
'A painstaking survey of English battlefields… a first-rate book' *Richard Holmes*
'A fascinating and, for all its factual tone, an atmospheric volume' *The Sunday Telegraph*

£18.99   978 07524 4307 2

Trafalgar Captain Durham of the Defiance: The Man who refused to Miss Trafalgar
HILARY RUBINSTEIN
'A sparkling biography of Nelson's luckiest captain' *Andrew Lambert*

£17.99   0 7524 3435 7

Battle of the Atlantic
MARC MILNER
'The most comprehensive short survey of the U-boat battles' *Sir John Keegan*
'Some events are fortunate in their historian, none more so than the Battle of the Atlantic. Marc Milner is *the* historian of the Atlantic Campaign… a compelling narrative'
Andrew Lambert

£12.99   0 7524 3332 6

Okinawa 1945 The Stalingrad of the Pacific
GEORGE FEIFER
'A great book… Feifer's account of the three sides and their experiences far surpasses most books about war' *Stephen Ambrose*

£17.99   0 7524 3324 5

Gallipoli 1915
TIM TRAVERS
'The most important new history of Gallipoli for forty years… groundbreaking' *Hew Strachan*
'A book of the highest importance to all who would seek to understand the tragedy of the Gallipoli campaign' *The Journal of Military History*

£13.99   0 7524 2972 8

Tommy Goes To War
MALCOLM BROWN
'A remarkably vivid and frank account of the British soldier in the trenches' *Max Arthur*
'The fury, fear, mud, blood, boredom and bravery that made up life on the Western Front are vividly presented and illustrated' *The Sunday Telegraph*

£12.99   0 7524 2980 9

TEMPUS – REVEALING HISTORY

Britannia's Empire
A Short History of the British Empire
BILL NASSON

'Crisp, economical and witty' *TLS*
'An excellent introduction the subject' *THES*

£12.99   0 7524 3808 5

Madmen
A Social History of Madhouses,
Mad-Doctors & Lunatics
ROY PORTER

'Fascinating'
The Observer

£12.99   0 7524 3730 5

Born to be Gay
A History of Homosexuality
WILLIAM NAPHY

'Fascinating' *The Financial Times*
'Excellent' *Gay Times*

£9.99   0 7524 3694 5

William II
Rufus, the Red King
EMMA MASON
'A thoroughly new reappraisal of a much
maligned king. The dramatic story of his life is
told with great pace and insight'
John Gillingham

£25   0 7524 3528 0

To Kill Rasputin
The Life and Death of Grigori Rasputin
ANDREW COOK

'Andrew Cook is a brilliant investigative historian'
Andrew Roberts
'Astonishing' *The Daily Mail*

£9.99   0 7524 3906 5

The Unwritten Order
Hitler's Role in the Final Solution
PETER LONGERICH

'Compelling' *Richard Evans*
'The finest account to date of the many twists
and turns in Adolf Hitler's anti-semitic obsession'
Richard Overy

£12.99   0 7524 3328 8

Private 12768
Memoir of a Tommy
JOHN JACKSON
FOREWORD BY HEW STRACHAN

'A refreshing new perspective' *The Sunday Times*
'At last we have John Jackson's intensely
personal and heartfelt little book to remind us
there was a view of the Great War other than
Wilfred Owen's' *The Daily Mail*

£9.99   0 7524 3531 0

The Vikings
MAGNUS MAGNUSSON

'Serious, engaging history'
BBC History Magazine

£9.99   0 7524 2699 0

If you are interested in purchasing other books published by Tempus, or in case you have difficulty finding any
Tempus books in your local bookshop, you can also place orders directly through our website

www.tempus-publishing.com

TEMPUS – REVEALING HISTORY

D-Day The First 72 Hours
WILLIAM F. BUCKINGHAM

'A compelling narrative' *The Observer*

A *BBC History Magazine* Book of the Year 2004

£9.99   0 7524 2842 x

The London Monster
Terror on the Streets in 1790
JAN BONDESON

'Gripping' *The Guardian*

'Excellent... monster-mania brought a reign of terror to the ill-lit streets of the capital' *The Independent*

£9.99   0 7524 3327 x

London
A Historical Companion
KENNETH PANTON

'A readable and reliable work of reference that deserves a place on every Londoner's bookshelf' *Stephen Inwood*

£20   0 7524 3434 9

M: MI5's First Spymaster
ANDREW COOK

'Serious spook history' *Andrew Roberts*

'Groundbreaking' *The Sunday Telegraph*

'Brilliantly researched' *Dame Stella Rimington*

£20   0 7524 2896 9

Agincourt A New History
ANNE CURRY

'A highly distinguished and convincing account' *Christopher Hibbert*

'A *tour de force*' *Alison Weir*

'*The* book on the battle' *Richard Holmes*

A *BBC History Magazine* Book of the Year 2005

£12.99   978 07524 3813 1

Battle of the Atlantic
MARC MILNER

'The most comprehensive short survey of the U-boat battles' *Sir John Keegan*

'Some events are fortunate in their historian, none more so than the Battle of the Atlantic. Marc Milner is *the* historian of the Atlantic campaign... a compelling narrative' *Andrew Lambert*

£12.99   0 7524 3332 6

The English Resistance
The Underground War Against the Normans
PETER REX

'An invaluable rehabilitation of an ignored resistance movement' *The Sunday Times*

'Peter Rex's scholarship is remarkable' *The Sunday Express*

£12.99   0 7524 3733 x

Elizabeth Wydeville: The Slandered Queen
ARLENE OKERLUND

'A penetrating, thorough and wholly convincing vindication of this unlucky queen' *Sarah Gristwood*

'A gripping tale of lust, loss and tragedy' *Alison Weir*

A *BBC History Magazine* Book of the Year 2005

£9.99   978 07524 3807 8

If you are interested in purchasing other books published by Tempus, or in case you have difficulty finding any Tempus books in your local bookshop, you can also place orders directly through our website

www.tempus-publishing.com

TEMPUS – REVEALING HISTORY

Quacks Fakers and Charlatans in Medicine
ROY PORTER

'A delightful book' *The Daily Telegraph*
'Hugely entertaining' *BBC History Magazine*

£12.99   0 7524 2590 0

The Tudors
RICHARD REX

'Up-to-date, readable and reliable. The best introduction to England's most important dynasty' *David Starkey*
'Vivid, entertaining... quite simply the best short introduction' *Eamon Duffy*
'Told with enviable narrative skill... a delight for any reader' *THES*

£9.99   0 7524 3333 4

The Kings & Queens of England
MARK ORMROD

'Of the numerous books on the kings and queens of England, this is the best' *Alison Weir*

£9.99   0 7524 2598 6

The Covent Garden Ladies
Pimp General Jack & the Extraordinary Story of Harris's List
HALLIE RUBENHOLD

'Sex toys, porn... forget Ann Summers, Miss Love was at it 250 years ago' *The Times*
'Compelling' *The Independent on Sunday*
'Marvellous' *Leonie Frieda*
'Filthy' *The Guardian*

£9.99   0 7524 3739 9

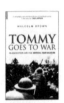

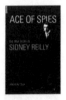

Okinawa 1945
GEORGE FEIFER

'A great book... Feifer's account of the three sides and their experiences far surpasses most books about war'
Stephen Ambrose

£17.99   0 7524 3324 5

Tommy Goes To War
MALCOLM BROWN

'A remarkably vivid and frank account of the British soldier in the trenches'
Max Arthur
'The fury, fear, mud, blood, boredom and bravery that made up life on the Western Front are vividly presented and illustrated'
The Sunday Telegraph

£12.99   0 7524 2980 4

Ace of Spies The True Story of Sidney Reilly
ANDREW COOK

'The most definitive biography of the spying ace yet written... both a compelling narrative and a myth-shattering *tour de force*'
Simon Sebag Montefiore
'The absolute last word on the subject' *Nigel West*
'Makes poor 007 look like a bit of a wuss'
The Mail on Sunday

£12.99   0 7524 2959 0

Sex Crimes
From Renaissance to Enlightenment
W.M. NAPHY

'Wonderfully scandalous'
Diarmaid MacCulloch

£10.99   0 7524 2977 9

Index